WESTMAR COLLEGE LIBRARY

W9-CBX-429

PESTALOZZI
&
EDUCATION

Studies in the
Western Educational Tradition

Consulting Editor
PAUL NASH · *Boston University*

PESTALOZZI
&
EDUCATION

Gerald Lee Gutek
· *Loyola University, Chicago* ·

RANDOM HOUSE · NEW YORK

92
P476g

LB
628
.G77

FIRST PRINTING

© Copyright, 1968, by Random House, Inc.

All rights reserved under
International and Pan-American Copyright Conventions.
Published in New York by Random House, Inc.
and simultaneously in Toronto, Canada,
by Random House of Canada Limited.

Library of Congress Catalog Card Number: 68–23001

Manufactured in the United States of America.
Printed by Halliday Lithograph Corp., West Hanover, Mass.
Bound by H. Wolff Book Manufacturing Co., New York, N. Y.

77928

Acknowledgment

*I wish to express appreciation to
Dean Richard A. Matre and
the Research Committee of Loyola University
for a grant that aided in
the preparation of the manuscript.*

G.L.G.

Contents

PESTALOZZI
&
EDUCATION

· I ·
The Climate
of Opinion

Although this book is an analysis of the theory and practice of the Swiss educator, Johann Heinrich Pestalozzi,
1747–1827, the narrative begins with the climate of opinion that existed in Switzerland during the latter half of
the eighteenth and the early years of the nineteenth centuries. Then, as now, Switzerland was a protected cross
section of Europe. The social, political, intellectual, and
economic currents sweeping post-Enlightenment Europe
had their effect on the Alpine cantons, which were a mo-
saic composed of rural-urban, feudal-democratic, Protestant-Catholic, and Teutonic-Romance conflicts.

Since his life, theories, and practices were a strange
conglomerate of forces and ideas, interpreters who seek

specific influences on Pestalozzi have stumbled into historical difficulties. If one struggles to sort out the various strands that comprised Pestalozzianism, there appears a bewildering tangle of diverse philosophical threads, such as Enlightenment rationalism, naturalistic romanticism, German idealism, pietistical Christianity, social philanthropism, political reformism, and industrial liberalism. It was a mixture rather than a blending. The reader who demands logical consistency will be disappointed by Pestalozzi's works. Rather than attempt to disentangle the influences that molded Pestalozzian educational theory, it is more discrete historically to refer to the climate of opinion that characterized the Swiss milieu during Pestalozzi's time.

POLITICAL MILIEU

Zurich, Pestalozzi's native city, was an important cultural center for the German-speaking Swiss. Although the formal political structure appeared to be a democratic city-state, a small clique of aristocratic families held actual power as a ruling oligarchy. Theocratically sanctioned by the reformed Zwinglian church, this old aristocracy repressed personal liberty and controlled the moral life of the city. Less powerful than the oligarchs some upper middle-class families also participated in public life. Guild membership, the qualification for citizenship, was restricted to these favored families.[1] An inheritance, guild membership, and citizenship were jealously guarded and passed on from father to son. Through these restrictions the oligarchy and their upper middle-class allies monopolized political and commercial power.

Although citizens, the Pestalozzi family was not part of the power structure of Zurich. Pestalozzi sympathized intensely with the poor country people who, although not actually tyrannized by the town, were often victimized by the corrupt bailiff system. His novel, *Leonard and Gertrude,* portrays such a situation where a fictional rural community, Bonnal, is victim of the malpractices of a dishonest bailiff.

In the canton of Zurich the farmers in the outlying rural districts were excluded from public affairs. These rural communities were administered by bailiffs appointed by the city government. Excluded from ministerial and governmental service the country people were restricted to manual work or to farming. Although sympathetic to the initial stage of the French Revolution, Pestalozzi did not recommend rebellion as an instrument for redressing grievances.

During his early career, Pestalozzi accepted enlightened despotism as a possible method for European political regeneration. Because of their familiarity with the doctrines of the Enlightenment, he naïvely hoped that rulers, such as Frederick II of Prussia and Catherine II of Russia, might paternalistically initiate reforms that would free the depressed masses. In particular Pestalozzi saw Joseph II of Austria as the father figure who would initiate a program of reformed natural education. Despite his beliefs in popular education and social equality, the Austrian monarch's reforms were as short-lived as was his reign. Although disappointed with the ineffective, half-hearted programs of the enlightened despots, Pestalozzi retained a belief that noble and paternalistic rulers would initiate programs of social and educational reform.

Since his hopes were ignored or rebuffed by the European aristocrats, Pestalozzi saw some possibility for reform in the new revolutionary French government. Experiencing mixed emotions about the overthrow of the Bourbons, Pestalozzi sympathized with the bourgeois stage of the revolution, which proclaimed the doctrines of Liberty, Equality, and Fraternity. He was enthusiastic about the proclamation of the Rights of Man, which to him expressed man's natural freedom. As a middle class liberal he could approve of the abolition of primogeniture, the freeing of the serfs, the confiscating of church lands, and the establishment of free trade. When the French National Assembly made him an honorary citizen of the republic along with George Washington, Thomas Paine, and Jeremy Bentham, Pestalozzi then accepted revolution and offered his educational services to the new government. The Committee on Public Instruction expressed interest in his educational theories, but failed to act on them. When the radical Jacobin seizure of power from the more conservative Girondists initiated the Reign of Terror, their excesses disgusted the gentle humanist, who had always distrusted the mass as a headless, irresponsible, and vicious monster. Preferring individual responsibility to mass action he recoiled from the bloody purges of Robespierre. After the reassertion of the middle class Directory in 1795 and the coming of Napoleon to power in 1799, Pestalozzi again hoped that France might perform an educational and civilizing mission. He was disappointed, however, when

Emperor Napoleon preferred empire-building to pedagogy.

Switzerland, like the rest of Europe, did not escape the revolutionary climate engendered by the events in France. In the wake of the French invasion of Switzerland in 1798 the country people of Zurich took advantage of the situation and forced the ruling oligarchs to grant them political rights and social equality. Despite the aristocratic capitulation the unsatisfied French demanded the total abolition of the old government. Spurred by external threat and internal pressure the revolutionary Helvetian Republic was proclaimed in 1798.

Serving as an intermediary between the aristocrats and the rebellious country people, Pestalozzi was not an active revolutionist. As a Swiss he resented foreign interference in the internal affairs of Zurich. As a humanitarian, however, he sympathized with the revolutionary principles and did not mourn the demise of control by the aristocratic oligarchy. As soon as the Helvetian Republic was proclaimed Pestalozzi determined to serve it in an educational capacity and applied for a teaching position. The Helvetian minister of education, P. A. Stapfer, accepted Pestalozzi's application and persuaded him to prepare a number of propaganda pamphlets for the new government.[2] Pestalozzi agreed to do so since he believed that the citizens of a republic needed a better education to perform the functions of self-government.

The proclamation of the republic left the Swiss political situation unsettled and the climate of opinion remained confused and chaotic. The Helvetian Republic really satisfied no one. The aristocrats were embittered by their loss of power and the peasants were unsatisfied because they never really gained control. The small group of middle class liberals who headed the Helvetian government were faced with chronic internal discontent, French interference, and an always empty treasury.

During the Napoleonic era the supporters of the Helvetian government sent Pestalozzi to Paris as a member of a deputation to win French support. Favoring a return to decentralization, Napoleon decreed the Mediation Act of 1803, which restored the independence of the nineteen Swiss cantons. Destroying the hopes of the Helvetian democratic centralists, this act restored the prerevolutionary status quo of domination by the aristocratic federalists.[3] This change in government caused Pestalozzi the loss of his political influence.

Napoleon's declining fortunes again affected Swiss politics. On their way to crush Napoleon, the allied armies invaded Switzerland and abrogated the enforced Mediation Act. Given the opportunity to choose their own governmental structure, the conservatives opted for federalism and their opponents wished to reassert centralization. Thus, Swiss politics remained in a state of uneasy truce between centralist and federalist during the remainder of Pestalozzi's life.

THE INTELLECTUAL CLIMATE

Pestalozzi was a child of the twin currents of intellectual thought that came from the European eighteenth-century Enlightenment: reason and romance. Both the rationalists and romanticists looked to nature for clues to the progressive development of the human race. The rationalists believed that men could free themselves from social evil and construct a better society of peace and perfection. Through the use of reason man could discover the natural laws regulating existence and in accordance with these universal laws he could ensure the progress of the human race.

Enlightenment thought embraced many diverse strands, but John Locke's *Essay Concerning Human Understanding* and Isaac Newton's *The Mathematical Principles of Natural Philosophy* were major sources of the Age of Reason. Although there is no evidence to indicate the direct influence of these works on Pestalozzi, they did contribute to the general climate that had an impact during his time. Denying the existence of innate ideas Locke's *Essay* asserted that the sources of man's ideas were in the experience of external sensible objects and the internal operations of the mind. The stress on sense experience was also a major point in Pestalozzi's writings. According to a recent interpretation given by Bayles and Hood:

> As is perhaps obvious, Pestalozzi's ABC of Anschauung, or Art of Sense Impressionism, is highly reminiscent of, if not identical with, the Aristotelian-Comenian-Lockean principle of tabula rasa with its principle that there is nothing in the mind except what is first received by way of the senses. Hence, in Pestalozzi we have a follower of Rousseau who espouses Lockean strategy.[4]

The Newtonian *Weltanschauung* conceived of the universe as a great world machine, which operated according to its own built-in laws and designs. In advocating the

scientific method, Newton believed that man could proceed by analysis to discover these natural laws that kept
the world in order and motion. Furthermore, it was possible to express these natural laws in mathematical terms
and to share them with all men. Although Newton, like
Darwin, was a natural scientist, social scientists believed
that the premises of natural law were equally applicable
to man's social life and institutions.

The Enlightenment coincided with a swing in the
pendulum of thought from a theocentric world view to
a humanistic one. Rejecting the old premise of man's innate corruption, the *philosophes* suggested instead that
man was naturally good and was capable of perfecting
himself through reason. With this optimistic faith in man's
propensity to goodness, the eighteenth-century intellectuals urged that manners, morals, governments, and institutions be rationally ordered in the light of nature. The
quest for a natural system of education was not unique to
Pestalozzi, but was part of the climate of opinion that
moved him to devote his life to the search.

In addition to rationalism, there was another force at
work, which was partly of the Enlightenment and partly
a prelude to nineteenth-century romanticism. This was
Rousseau's romantic naturalism, which is cited by vir-
tually all of Pestalozzi's interpreters as a source of influence. According to Mayer:

> *Pestalozzi reflected the influence of Rousseau and roman-*
> *ticism. Like Rousseau, Pestalozzi stressed the natural de-*
> *velopment of the child and, like Rousseau, Pestalozzi had*
> *great distrust for authoritarianism in education.*[5]

In referring to the influence of Rousseau's educational novel, *Emile,* 1762, upon him, Pestalozzi said, ". . . my visionary and highly speculative mind was enthusiastically seized by this visionary and highly speculative book." [6] According to Rousseau man is naturally good but is corrupted by artificial institutions, traditions, customs, and laws. Rousseau dealt with the problem of developing an education that would permit the child's natural goodness to develop in the midst of a pernicious social environment.[7] In rejecting a verbal and literary education Emile was educated according to nature. Rousseau's treatise contained numerous principles that were included by Pestalozzi in his own novel, *Leonard and Gertrude,* and in subsequent works. The following Rousseauean principles seem to have had an impact on Pestalozzi: (1) man is naturally good; (2) evil lies in a corruptive social environment rather than in nature; (3) education can be instrumental in blocking the distortions of an unnatural environment and in allowing the child to develop according to his natural goodness; (4) human growth proceeds gradually according to well-defined stages; (5) sensation, rather than verbalism, is the true basis of ideas; (6) the natural environment is a plentious source of educative experiences.

Pestalozzi followed Rousseau's condemnation of the unnatural, the artificial. However he was not led to a rejection of society or to a completely naturalistic religion. His acceptance of Rousseau's admonition to return to nature brought him to the country people and to agriculture. Pestalozzi was acquainted with the works of the French physiocrats who developed an economic theory based on their conception of natural law. For an eight-month period in 1767, Pestalozzi worked with the physiocratic Swiss agriculturalist, Tschiffeli. The climate of opinion included the doctrines of François Quesnay and the school of physiocratic economists who held land to be the sole source of wealth and agriculture to be the only means of increasing wealth. Opposing mercantilism, Quesnay argued against equating money with wealth and against interference with the natural economic laws. Although Quesnay and Adam Smith disagreed as to the source of wealth, both stressed the liberalism that opposed governmental interference with the natural law of supply and demand. Thus Pestalozzi was a part of that cultural milieu that grew out of the Enlightenment of the eighteenth century.

THE EDUCATIONAL CLIMATE

During the eighteenth and early nineteenth centuries, formal education persisted in its perennial error of ignoring intellectual and social change. Although the ideas of Locke, Rousseau, and Montaigne stimulated European intellectuals, the conventional schools resisted the enticements of the Enlightenment in favor of classical learning, which, although exciting in the Renaissance, had now grown cold. Although Basedow, Francke, and Condorcet might urge pedagogical reformation, schoolmasters persisted in stressing discipline and memorization. Thus many of the schools still merited the name "slaughter houses of the mind" given them by Comenius.

The elementary schools remained primarily reading

schools that stressed basic literacy, writing, singing, and arithmetic in addition to emphasizing religious conformity and commitment. The various and conflicting denominations had not yet forgotten nor forgiven the contentions of the Reformation. Children were admonished to defend their particular faith by memorizing catechisms, psalters, primers, and creeds. Schoolmasters were still school keepers rather than teachers and were employed on the basis of both their religious conformity and skill in maintaining discipline. Thus, the heavy-handed, incompetent bigot was often preferred to the educated man for teaching positions.

The various secondary schools, the German *gymnasium,* the French *lycée,* and the English grammar school, were somewhat more responsive to the currents of the Enlightenment than the elementary schools. In Germany Francke succeeded in enriching the classical school curriculum by adding scientific and natural studies. Although the English grammar school remained anchored to classical studies, Latin, Greek, and theology, some of the dissenter academies also included English, natural sciences, and physical sciences. However, the secondary school curriculum was still dominated by pedagogical devotion to Latin and Greek as the necessary marks of the educated man. In higher education professional preparation in theology, law, or medicine was the dominant pursuit and the Catholic scholastic, the Protestant classical humanist, and the Enlightenment scholar struggled for places in the university. Generally speaking institutions of formal education were not the most exciting places in the post-Enlightenment era.

THE RELIGIOUS CLIMATE

During the life of Pestalozzi, the legally established state churches in Europe retained those powers that had been either reaffirmed or won during the Protestant Reformation and the Catholic counter-Reformation. In Italy, Spain, France, and the Holy Roman Empire, the Roman Catholic Church maintained power. In France, of course, the fortunes of Catholicism, as the state church, depended upon twists and turns of the revolution. Catholicism was restored as the official religion by Napoleon. In England Anglicanism reigned supreme. On the European continent the two major Protestant covenants, Lutheranism and Calvinism, were recognized as the state churches in the non-Catholic countries. For example, the Netherlands, some of the German states, and some of the Swiss cantons were Calvinist. Religious establishment was one of the dominant characteristics of eighteenth-century Europe.

The Swiss cantons were either predominantly Catholic or reformed according to Zwinglian-Calvinist theology. Geneva had once been a kind of Calvinist Rome from which had emanated a major theological current of the Reformation. In Pestalozzi's canton, Zurich, the Zwinglian-Calvinist church was established.

The eighteenth century also experienced a religious and evangelical phenomenon referred to as the "great awakening." Numerous new religious organizations that were neither Calvinist, Lutheran, nor Catholic came into existence. Mennonites, Quakers, Baptists, Amish, Dunkers, Millerites, and others splintered off from the major Christian churches to become fully independent denominations. Unlike the Catholics, Calvinists, and Lutherans, many of these pietistical Christian denominations advocated a religion of the heart rather than a carefully constructed intellectualistic theology. The Pietism of the religion of the heart was also a part of the Swiss milieu and traces of it were found in Pestalozzi's educational methodology.

In discussing the religious climate in Zurich, Silber has contrasted Pietism with the Zwinglian state church. While the Zwinglians emphasized doctrinal conformity and theological rigidity, the Pietists cultivated personal religious experience and individual Bible study. For the Zwinglian Calvinists material prosperity signified providential approval. In contrast the Pietists who stressed meditation and simplicity attached no spiritual significance to property.[8] Pietism's affirmation of the good-hearted man coincided with Pestalozzi's emphasis on the priority of the moral values.

It is difficult to identify precisely Pestalozzi's particular form of religion. He had been educated in the general tradition of reformed Protestantism. Pestalozzi did not break openly with this heritage and occasionally used its language to express his educational theory. In assimilating the naturalism of the Enlightenment, Silber indicates that Pestalozzi combined both the tradition of reformed Christianity and the natural religion of Rousseau and the other *philosophes*.[9] As a result Pestalozzi was a naturalistic Christian humanist who held that while the powers of human nature were God given it was man's responsibility to cooperate with nature and thus ensure his own self-improvement, or his own natural salvation.

ECONOMIC CONDITIONS

Pestalozzi's life coincided with the transition from an essentially agrarian economy to an industrial one. Cottage work, or handicraft production, was the first step in European industrialization. It is significant that cottage industry persisted in Switzerland along with agricultural and factory industry. Swiss working classes, both farmers and factory operatives, were forced to cope with a wage economy. These new economic conditions required a more sophisticated education. Pestalozzi sought to foster more adequate agricultural training, domestic management, and industrial workmanship. He said:

> The means to be employed for the salvation of the fatherland seemed clearly discernible and practicable. I believed that I could neutralize the most oppressive consequences of the evils of the feudal system and of the factory system through renewed effort for the education of the people to increased productivity in home and farm work and to a greater degree of self-respect.[10]

Pestalozzi's acceptance of Enlightenment naturalism led him to accept agriculture as a major human occupation that permitted man to be near nature. His earliest educational venture at Neuhof was essentially agricultural, and gardening always had a place as a valuable educative experience in his institutions. During the eighteenth century farming was inadequate to sustain the population growth and the rural, agricultural classes were impoverished. The revolutionary and Napoleonic wars had further debilitated the population. The physiocratic doctrines of land wealth held out the promise that through scientific agriculture a real prosperity could be restored. In accepting these doctrines Pestalozzi believed that through education the agricultural population could be morally, socially, and economically regenerated.

Although agriculture remained a major concern of Pestalozzi, he was also well aware of the impact of the industrial age. The initial phase of the industrial revolution, from about 1776 to 1850, had brought about a social dehumanization of the workingman. Educated gentlemen, such as Pestalozzi, who had been nurtured in the classical humanist tradition of the preindustrial period, found this tendency to dehumanization particularly distressing. Beck places Pestalozzi in the context of the reformer who sought to ameliorate and improve human conditions through educational reformation.[11]

The major dehumanizing characteristics of the early factory system resulted from the mechanical and monotonous work that was performed. The specialized routines of factory work destroyed the pride of workmanship, or craftsmanship, which had characterized home industries. Despite these negative effects industrialization was making possible a higher standard of living. Pestalozzi did not feel that the industrial revolution could or should be reversed. With more money and more consumer products available, men needed a more sophisticated education to benefit fully from higher wages. Men had to be educated to work skillfully and to desire those things that aided natural development rather than those that impeded it.

Early industrialization was especially detrimental to the condition of the family. To make a living whole families entered the factory and worked long hours. Parents and children might be together for only short periods of the day. As the home disintegrated as the occupational core, instances of child neglect increased. The growing rates of child delinquency nurtured the concept that the working class was by nature vicious and depraved. The doctrine of child depravity now had two supports: (1) the Calvinist concept that the child was born in sin and naturally corrupt; (2) the concept born during the industrial revolution that the working class, as the dregs of society, produced children who were vicious, idle, and mean. Pestalozzi, like Rousseau, believed in the natural goodness of the child. Recognizing that children were being physically, mentally, and morally ruined by the factory system, Pestalozzi felt that unwholesome traits were caused by environmental factors that greedy and narrow-minded employers forced upon the workers. With natural education all children were capable of developing into morally respectable, economically self-sufficient, and socially useful adults.[12]

Beck has distinguished three major impulses of educational reform in the period from the seventeenth through the late nineteenth centuries. The first impulse was humanitarian and sought aid and charity for the children of the poor and instruction of orphans, delinquents, and pauper children in marketable skills, such as weaving and spinning. The second impulse was nonphilanthropic and emphasized vocational education as appropriate for children who would work after completing primary schooling. The third impulse conceived of manual training as a sound general education in disciplining the mind, hand, and character.[13]

Pestalozzian educational theory and practice embraced all three impulses. Primarily concerned with the education of poor children Pestalozzi believed that there was an appropriate kind of vocational education for the different socioeconomic classes. Believing vocational education to be part of total education, he urged that it be subordinated to general and harmonious development in the broader context of natural education.

Pestalozzi recognized the impact of industrialization on home life and child growth and development. Although he was aware that a new period in history was being ushered in, he did not fully realize the broader implications of the industrial revolution. He tried to cope with its immediate effects as it touched upon the lives of children. He was not a social planner or a social reconstructionist, but rather he was the educator who preferred to work with individual children.

Like all men, Pestalozzi was touched by the major political, intellectual, religious, educational, and economic currents of his time. He was part of that cultural milieu that experienced the political revolution of Liberty, Equality, and Fraternity, and the economic revolution of industrialism. He knew both the intellectual stimulation of the Enlightenment and the emotionalism of romanticism and Pietism. Despite the storms and stresses of his time he retained an optimism that man was capable of self-perfection. This belief motivated Johann Heinrich Pestalozzi to work among the poor, to develop an educational theory, and to devote his life to man's betterment. The following chapter is devoted to a consideration of Pestalozzi's lifelong search for a natural system of education that was capable of aiding man in his struggle for self-perfection.

· NOTES ·

1. Kate Silber, *Pestalozzi: The Man and His Work* (London: Routledge and Kegan Paul, 1960), pp. 1–2.
2. *Ibid.*, pp. 108–109.
3. *Ibid.*, pp. 155–156.
4. Ernest E. Bayles and Bruce L. Hood, *Growth of American Educational Thought and Practice* (New York: Harper & Row, 1966), p. 106.
5. Frederick Mayer, *American Ideas and Education* (Columbus, Ohio: Merrill, 1964), pp. 156–157.
6. Johann H. Pestalozzi, *How Gertrude Teaches Her Children,* trans. L. E. Holland and F. C. Turner (Syracuse: Bardeen, 1900), p. xvi.
7. For an excellent essay on Rousseau's educational theory, see Stanley E. Ballinger, "The Natural Man: Rousseau," in Paul Nash, Andreas M. Kazamias, and Henry J. Perkinson, eds., *The Educated Man* (New York: Wiley, 1965), pp. 224–246.
8. Silber, *op. cit.*, p. 2.
9. *Ibid.*, p. 17.
10. Johann H. Pestalozzi, "Views and Experiences," in Lewis F. Anderson, ed., *Pestalozzi* (New York: McGraw-Hill, 1931), p. 101.
11. Robert H. Beck, *A Social History of Education* (Englewood Cliffs, N.J.: Prentice-Hall, 1965), p. 74.
12. I. N. Thut, *The Story of Education: Philosophical and Historical Foundations* (New York: McGraw-Hill, 1957), p. 234.
13. Beck, *op. cit.*, p. 75.

· II ·
Johann Heinrich Pestalozzi: Life and Work

FAMILY ORIGINS

Johann Heinrich Pestalozzi was born in Zurich, Switzerland, on January 12, 1746, into a middle class Protestant family of Italian origin. His great grandfather, Johann Pestalozzi, had emigrated from Chivaenna to Zurich where he married Madgalene von Muralt. From this union was born Andreas Pestalozzi who was the father of Johann Baptiste and the grandfather of Johann Heinrich. A physician and surgeon, Johann Baptiste married Susanna Hotz. Pestalozzi's parents had three surviving children, Johann Baptiste, Anna Barbara, and Johann Heinrich. Pestalozzi's father died in 1751, at the age of thirty-three, leaving the Pestalozzi family with little financial support.

After his father's death Pestalozzi's mother, Susanna,

came to rely on the family servant, Barbara Schmid, for advice in managing the family's affairs. Known as Babeli by the family, this servant effected stringent economies on the household. Pestalozzi's mother was a shy woman who had few social contacts outside her family. Babeli, who was strong willed, came to assert a dominant influence on young Pestalozzi. Babeli prevented the children from peer group contact; thus, Pestalozzi grew up as a socially isolated child much given to daydreams and fantasies. Despite his own sheltered childhood, Pestalozzi extolled "love, work and social intercourse" as man's natural means of developing his human powers.[1]

Pestalozzi's boyhood was spent in a house ruled by women. He complained in later life that this feminine environment had made him shy, ill at ease, and socially incompetent. He felt that his inability to make a financial success of his ventures resulted from the impractical daydreams of his isolated childhood. Critical of the childhood that had tied him to his mother's apron strings, he complained that he had no experience in playing with boys of his own age: "I knew none of their games, their exercises, their secrets; naturally, I was awkward in their midst and the object of their ridicule." [2]

Despite these deficiencies of his childhood, Pestalozzi praised his "noble and dedicated" mother and the devoted family servant. He felt that this gentle femininity had exerted an influence that enabled him to sympathize with the poor and destitute. Although he felt that his childhood had left him an impractical visionary, Pestalozzi also claimed that it fostered in him attitudes of benevolence, kindliness, and sympathy. In his later educational works

Pestalozzi always used a feminine figure as a means of personifying his educational method.

As a child Pestalozzi's sole source of masculine influence was his grandfather, Andreas Pestalozzi, who was pastor at Hongg, a rural village, in the canton of Zurich. Pastor Pestalozzi ministered in the local church and taught in the village school. Occasionally young Johann Heinrich would accompany the pastor on his visits to peasant homes. The Swiss farmers were usually poor and were deprived of the political and social prerogatives enjoyed by their city neighbors. Pestalozzi gained a sympathy for these farmers who were usually victimized by absentee land-lords and the city bureaucrats who served as politically appointed bailiffs in the rural areas.

PESTALOZZI'S OWN EDUCATION

Pestalozzi received a conventional education in the Zurich schools. After attending a vernacular elementary school for three years, he entered the Schola Abbatissana in 1754 and then in 1757 transferred to the Schola Carolina. Both institutions were classical Latin schools that offered college preparatory subjects. With the completion of secondary studies Pestalozzi entered the two-year program of the Collegium Humanitatis, which offered a curriculum of Latin, Greek, Hebrew, rhetoric, logic, and catechetics.[3] The humanities curriculum was designed to prepare students for professional careers in theology, medicine, or law. After completing the two-year humanities program the seventeen-year-old Pestalozzi entered the Collegium Carolinum where he studied philology and philosophy. As a college student the hitherto sheltered youth became part of an intellectual group of professors and students who were interested in the restoration of Swiss life and liberty. Three professors seemed to have made a special impression on Pestalozzi during his college career: the theology professor, Zimmerman, the Greek and Hebrew professor, Breitinger, and the professor of Swiss history and politics, Bodmer. In addition to teaching their subject specialities, these men performed the task of social criticism and urged the regeneration of the Swiss virtues of freedom, justice, simplicity, and self-sacrifice.

Jean Jacques Bodmer, 1699–1773, seems to have exerted a significant influence over his students. His lectures in history and political economy included examinations of Swiss social and economic conditions. In addition to his historical interests Bodmer was a literary critic and poet. Stressing the German style he opposed the imitation of the French style of writing by German authors. His works were translations of Homer and Milton, a volume of *Critical Letters,* and *Collections from the Minnesingers.* Bodmer's point of view emphasized an affirmation of the classical Spartan life with the romantic folk literature and spirit of the old Swiss mountaineers. He urged his students to resist the softness of contemporary life and manners and to live according to the old Swiss values of simplicity and liberty. Bodmer's advocacy of "plain living and high thinking" blended classicism and romanticism.[4] Most significant as an influence on Pestalozzi was Bodmer's insistence that Swiss regeneration could begin only in the simple folk home. In developing his educational theory Pestalozzi reaffirmed the crucial importance of the home circle as the origin of all education.

In 1765 Bodmer founded the Helvetic Society, a youth movement intended to elevate Swiss morality. Through the discussion of historical, educational, political, and social issues, the national rebirth was to occur. Probably through their founder's influence, the Helvetians drew their inspiration from a blend of classical asceticism and the romanticism that urged a return to nature. Pestalozzi joined the Helvetic Society and made close friendships with his fellow members, Johann Caspar Fussli, Caspar Schulthess, Johann Bluntschli, and Johann Lavater.[5] The Helvetians sought to engender Swiss regeneration through literature and education rather than through revolution. The group published a weekly journal, *The Monitor,* to which Pestalozzi contributed a number of articles. In urging social reform, *The Monitor* attacked some of the political abuses and corruption in Zurich. The journal was suppressed and Pestalozzi and some of his associates were jailed for three days in the town hall.

Because of his affiliation with the Helvetians, Pestalozzi was branded as a dangerous radical. This held some interesting implications for his career. At first he wanted to be a minister like his grandfather. Although he did some preparation for the ministry and went as far as to preach a trial sermon, he decided to pursue a legal rather than a theological career. The law seemed to have possibilities for remedying the political and economic inequalities faced by the poor. However Pestalozzi's association with the Helvetians blocked his admittance to the legal profession. He gave up further study and left the Collegium without taking a final degree.

In his later life, Pestalozzi was critical of his classical education and his youthful political activities. His formal education, he felt, had prepared him no better than his childhood for the real world of practical work. Further, he believed that the Swiss academicians were too theoretical as reformers and had neglected to fashion a practical program to achieve social regeneration. In reacting to his education Pestalozzi reminisced:

> *Our only wish was to live for freedom, beneficence, sacrifice and patriotism; but the means of developing the practical power to attain these were lacking. We despised all external appearances such as riches, honour, and consideration; and we were taught to believe that by economising and reducing our wants we could dispense with all the advantages of citizen life. We cherished but one aim namely, the possibility of enjoying independence and domestic happiness, without having the strength to acquire and maintain them.*[6]

AGRICULTURAL APPRENTICESHIP

After leaving formal studies Pestalozzi decided to turn to an agricultural career. Impressed by Rousseau's writings on a return to nature and by Helvetian romanticizing of peasant virtues, he considered agriculture a desirable pursuit. In September 1767 Pestalozzi went to Johann Rudolf Tschiffeli's experimental farm, near Kirchberg in the canton of Berne, for training in the principles of scientific farming. Tschiffeli was well known for his success in raising madder, clover, and potatoes. Pestalozzi believed that he could emulate Tschiffeli's successful venture. He was unaware that the experimental farm was not economically self-sustaining but was largely supported by Tschiffeli's private income.[7] Lacking practical business acumen Pestalozzi became enthusiastic about combining his ideals of Swiss social regeneration with the physiocratic doctrines of land value as the basis of real wealth. Pestalozzi developed a plan by which the Swiss people would, through improved agricultural production, live in greater economic independence and provide for the intellectual and moral regeneration of their children. By a return to nature and to the soil the farm family might be restored as the moral center of Swiss life.

Pestalozzi resolved to establish an experimental farm that would be so prosperous and well managed that it could serve as a model for other Swiss farmers. He secured a loan and purchased sixty acres of land near the village of Birr in the canton of Berne. On this farm Pestalozzi planned to raise madder and to engage in cotton spinning. Now a property owner, Pestalozzi ended his long courtship, married Anna Schulthess, a daughter of one of the respected upper middle-class families of Zurich. On September 30, 1769, the marriage took place after Anna's parents gave their reluctant consent. Anna Schulthess was born in 1738 and was eight years older than her husband. She has been described as a patient, attractive, and capable woman. During the early years of their marriage Anna was able to give Pestalozzi practical assistance in managing their affairs. During their later years Anna's health failed and she was given to long periods of religious contemplation, which isolated her from many of her husband's educational experiments.

Anna and Johann Heinrich Pestalozzi had one child, Jean Jacques, who was born on August 18, 1770. Jacobli, as he was called, was a physically and mentally weak child who suffered from an illness that has been described as "violent rheumatism." Most likely, he was an epileptic. Nevertheless, Pestalozzi held high hopes for his son and he attempted to apply some of the educational ideas from Rousseau's *Emile* to his upbringing. When Jacobli was three years old Pestalozzi kept a diary of his educational progress. De Guimps has quoted some excerpts from this diary:

January 27, 1774.

I showed him the water which ran rapidly down the slope of the hill. He was delighted with this. As we went down the hill he said, "Look papa, the water comes too, it comes from above, and it always goes lower." We followed the course of the water and I repeated to him several times "the water flows from the top to the bottom of the mountain."

February 19.

Whatever you can teach him from the nature of things themselves, do not teach him by words. Leave him to himself to see, hear, find, stumble, rise again, and be mistaken. Give no words when action, or deed is possible. What he can do for himself let him do. Let him be always occupied, ever active, and let the time when you do not worry him be by far the greatest part of his childhood. You will come to learn that nature teaches him better than men.[8]

Although still convinced of the efficacy of natural education, Pestalozzi's experiences in the education of his son led him to discover some inadequacies in Rousseau's advice. At the age of eleven Jacobli was still unable to read or to write. Pestalozzi believed that Rousseau had failed to articulate the pedagogical principles that were needed to teach the basic skills of reading, writing, and arithmetic. Jacobli's formal schooling was as unsuccessful as was his apprenticeship to a merchant friend. Frequently ill, Jacobli reached manhood and married Anna Froelich. The couple had several children but only one survived. Jean Jacques died in 1800 at the age of thirty.[9]

NEUHOF

By 1771 Pestalozzi had settled his wife and son in his recently purchased estate, Neuhof. After three years of relying solely on farming for a livelihood, he decided to add a spinning mill to the farm and to found an institution for poor children that would combine work and learning. Pestalozzi officially opened his school in 1774. He gathered together pauper children from the nearby villages and clothed and fed them. From time to time the children would leave the institution taking their new wardrobes with them. The experiment was a constant drain on Pestalozzi's finances and he tried to raise money by public appeal to "the friends and benefactors of humanity wishing to support an establishment intended to give education and work to poor country children." [10]

Although Pestalozzi was now sure of his choice of career as an educator, he found himself handicapped not only by lack of money but also by an inadequate knowl-

edge of educational theory and practice. Pestalozzi's experiment at Neuhof was based on the two major theories of
self-activity and economic independence. Believing it natural for children to be active, the educator provided children with a variety of exercises that contained vocational,
moral, and intellectual possibilities for growth and development. Sympathetic to the poverty of the peasant class,
he believed that self-respect and economic independence
were related to vocational skill. Instead of relying on a
dole that perpetuated poverty, poor children should be educated to self-reliance.

Pestalozzi attempted to base his institutional program in
home education. He accommodated fifty boys and girls
ranging in age from six to eighteen years. During the
summer the children did field work to learn agricultural
skills. During the winter they spun and engaged in other
handicrafts associated with cottage industry. While working, the children were given lessons in arithmetic, religion,
and morality. The chief means of instruction was the
group recitation, which occurred as the children worked
either in the fields or at the spinning wheel. In addition,
Pestalozzi tried to provide lessons in reading and writing.
The girls practiced domestic skills of cooking and sewing.
Master spinners and weavers were employed to teach their
skills to the boys and girls.

A gentle person, Pestalozzi wanted his institution to re-
semble a family rather than either a workshop or school.
Based on the assumption that the educational family
unit should work and learn together, Pestalozzi hoped to
preside as a father figure in a love atmosphere that would
achieve both humanitarian and vocational ends. Unfortunately Neuhof was not a financial success. The expenses

greatly exceeded the profits and the school was forced to close in 1779. Pestalozzi believed that his working premises were sound, but that the failure resulted from his ineptitude as a business administrator and the hostility of an unsympathetic community. Neuhof revealed a weakness that would plague all of Pestalozzi's subsequent educational institutions. He was pathetically inept as an administrator.

In reflecting upon his first experiment at Neuhof, Pestalozzi was nostalgic about his initial effort, which was "permeated by the spirit of a well-ordered home." [11] He believed throughout his life that Neuhof had put him on the right pathway, which eventually led him to articulate his philosophy of natural education.

At Neuhof Pestalozzi had his first real working relationship with the poverty-ridden whom he wanted to rescue from their degraded condition. In working with these economically and culturally deprived individuals, Pestalozzi found himself in the same position as many middle class reformers who deal with people that they do not yet understand. Both the parents and the children regarded Pestalozzi with suspicion. They felt that he was trying to use them for his own profit. Parents cooperated with Pestalozzi only to the extent of having their children fed and clothed and then they encouraged their children to leave the school. As a result of the experiment at Neuhof Pestalozzi had depleted his investment and his wife's inheritance.

In writing about Neuhof, a nineteenth-century German educator, Karl Blochmann, took Pestalozzi to task for the inconsistencies between theory and practice that occurred in this initial experiment. Blochmann accused Pestalozzi of pushing the children into technical manufacturing skills without giving them knowledge of basic skills:

> . . . *he hurried on to the higher branches of instruction, before supplying the solid foundation of acquaintance with the lower; an error recognized as the leading one of the teaching of the age, against which he had striven in his scheme of education with all his strength. For the sake of a fallacious prospect of great profit, in higher branches of industry, he committed, in teaching his children to spin and weave, the very faults which he had so strongly abjured in all his expressed opinions upon education, and which he saw to be so dangerous to children of all classes. He would attempt to secure the finest spinning, before his children had acquired even a small amount of firmness and surety of hand in coarse work. . . .*[12]

Although Blochmann's criticisms of Pestalozzi's inabilities as a financial and educational administrator are undoubtedly valid, some of the alleged practical violations of theory are too harsh. Pestalozzi was just beginning his educational career and had not yet arrived at his theory of natural education with its attendant principles of *Anschauung* and gradual development. Much theorizing needed to be done before Pestalozzi would arrive at his psychologizing of instruction.

THE LITERARY PERIOD

Pestalozzi lost control of most of his estate at Neuhof, but he retained possession of the house where he lived until he resumed his educational experimentation by accepting a headmastership of a poor school at Stans in 1798. Financially destitute, Pestalozzi was the subject of ridicule by acquaintances, some of whom predicted that he was destined for a lunatic asylum. During this troubled period Pestalozzi's close friend Isaac Iselin persuaded him to write to earn a living for his family. The years from 1780 to 1798 were the period of his most significant contributions to educational literature. During these eighteen years of exile from educational practice Pestalozzi articulated his natural philosophy of education.

In 1774 Pestalozzi published a short work, *How Father Pestalozzi Instructed His Three and a Half Year Old Son,* and wrote several appeals for funds to support experiments at Neuhof in Iselin's journal, *Ephemerides.* From 1775 to 1778 these appeals appeared as *Essays on the Education of the Children of the Poor,* but failed to attract the needed benefactors. *The Evening Hours of a Hermit* appeared in installments in *Ephemerides* during this same period. *The Evening Hours* consisted of 180 aphorisms, such as:

> All the pure and beneficent powers of humanity are neither the product of art, nor the effects of chance. They exist virtually in the inmost nature of all men. Their development is a great need of humanity.[13]

Pestalozzi failed to attract attention as a writer until the publication of his educational novel, *Leonard and Gertrude,* in 1781. So successful was this work that revised editions appeared in 1783, 1785, and 1787. Bringing fame to its author, the novel earned Pestalozzi the gold medal award of the Economic Society of Berne and a gift of fifty florins. Like Rousseau's *Emile*, *Leonard and Gertrude* was intended to show the world that social regeneration was possible through education. The novel was widely read as a romantic novel and most of the readers neglected its educational significance.

Despite its abundance of eighteenth-century romantic sentimentalism, *Leonard and Gertrude* clearly revealed both the personality and the theory of its author. The scene of the novel is the fictional village of Bonnal, which is much like the village of Hongg where Pestalozzi visited his grandfather's parish. As in Hongg the villagers were exploited by the bailiff, Hummel, who is also the village tavern keeper. The new economic innovation of cotton spinning brought the villagers an increased amount of money. In taking advantage of the villagers' ignorance as workers and consumers, the evil bailiff, Hummel, controlled the life of Bonnal through a network of lies, deceit, fear, and bribery.

Pestalozzi used Gertrude as the mother figure who initiated the regeneration of the village. Gertrude's weak-willed husband, Leonard, is the village mason. Although a good craftsman, Leonard was deluded by the wiles of the crafty bailiff and became financially indebted to him. In desperation Gertrude enlisted the aid of the young aristocrat, Arner, who is the absentee landlord of the village. Through the character of Arner, Pestalozzi revealed his faith in the enlightened paternalism of the landed or titled aristocracy. Once the young aristocrat was made aware of the conditions in Bonnal, he became concerned and desired to aid in the regeneration of the lower socio-economic class. Pestalozzi's choice of a title for chapter two revealed his faith in the power of woman and paternalistic reform: "A Woman Who Forms a Resolution, Acts Up to It, and Finds a Lord of the Manor, Who has the Heart of a Father Toward His Dependents." [14]

The forces of good in Bonnal are represented by Arner, the village pastor, and the schoolmaster, who rally around Gertrude. The model of educational and social reform is found in the home of Gertrude, the perfect working class housewife and mother. As the first teacher of her children she trained them through their senses and guided their observation of nature. She also trained them in the work activities that contributed to the family's economic well-being. Through the example of Gertrude the villagers learn that genuine regeneration will come about only through natural education. Based on the principle of home education, the school begins to function as the moral, intellectual, and vocational heart of the village, which is morally and economically restored.

This simple novel, *Leonard and Gertrude,* is basic to an understanding of the Pestalozzian philosophy of education. The following essential doctrines of natural education are directly outlined for the reader: (1) the source of evil lies in a distorted environment; (2) men may be ignorant, but they are capable of regeneration; (3) the true road to social reform lies in the peaceful processes of education; (4) genuine education cooperates in the development of man's natural moral, intellectual, and physical powers; (5) human development begins in the home circle and the child responds with gratitude to the loving care of the mother; (6) true education will produce economically self-sufficient individuals.

In 1782 Pestalozzi published *Christopher and Elizabeth*, a series of dialogues in which the family of Christopher gathers about the hearth to discuss their reading of *Leonard and Gertrude*. This work was a dull didactic and failed to attract any significant attention. During the years 1782–1783 Pestalozzi also published a paper of his own, *Ein Schweizer Blatt*, the *Swiss News*. He wrote a number of articles that stressed the importance of the home as the center of education and attacked the verbalistic, artificial state of contemporary education. Like *Christopher and Elizabeth*, this journal was ignored and Pestalozzi was forced to discontinue its publication. In 1783 he wrote an essay, *On Legislation and Infanticide*, which examined the relationships between environment, crime, punishment, education, traditions, and morals. In 1787 he published *Illustrations for My ABC Book*, which was intended to provide a number of short illustrative epilogues on morality, society, and education as an accompaniment to *Leonard and Gertrude*. A second edition of this work appeared in 1795 under the title, *Fables For My ABC*.

In 1797 Pestalozzi attempted to establish a strong theoretical foundation for his pedagogical efforts in the publication of *Researches Into the Course of Nature in the Development of the Human Race*. Although the book failed to attract attention and was a disappointment to its author, *Researches* was significant in that it was one of the first attempts to produce a sociology of education. Pestalozzi's thesis was that knowledge of the natural patterns of development would enlighten all ethical and political science and supply man with a solid educational base. Human progress depended upon man's effort to elevate himself to the moral state through an education motivated by love and understanding. Very critical of his own work, Pestalozzi condemned it as impractical, abstract, and vague. In reference to *Researches,* Pestalozzi said:

> The influence of my book around me was the same as the influence of all that I had done. Nobody understood me and I did not meet two men who did not let me know that they considered the whole work as nonsense.[15]

In 1798 the struggling young Helvetian Republic sought to establish a journalistic organ that would be favorable to the new government. Pestalozzi was appointed editor of *The Popular Swiss Gazette,* which was to appear weekly and serve as a source of information to ministers, teachers, and public officials who were to read and explain it. The paper failed to have its desired effect and the government ceased its publication after nineteen issues. During the same year Pestalozzi accepted a call as director of an orphanage and poor school at Stans. This marked his return to practice after spending eighteen years in writing and theorizing.

Before returning to Pestalozzi's major educational experiments at Stans, Burgdorf, and Yverdon, three other major works should be discussed. The writing of *How Gertrude Teaches Her Children,* 1801, *Pestalozzi to His Age,* or *Epochs,* 1802–1803, and his final work, *Swansong,* 1826, took place during the long years of educational experimentation from 1798 until his death in 1827.

How Gertrude Teaches Her Children was written in the form of fourteen letters to Gessner, Pestalozzi's publisher in Zurich. It is a confusing book in terms of its organization; it combines autobiographical and personal accounts with detailed exposition of Pestalozzi's theory of natural education. Pestalozzi apologized for his inability to express himself clearly and for his failure to make his educational concepts into clearly defined philosophical principles. He remarked that he much preferred the role of educational experimenter to that of philosopher.[16] Despite these weaknesses *How Gertrude Teaches Her Children* is an important articulation of natural education based on the harmonious development of man's moral, intellectual, and physical powers.

The essay, *Pestalozzi to His Age,* reiterated the thesis that man could restore himself to the state of natural goodness through education. *Swansong* recounted his views on elementary education. Unfortunately, much of the work was devoted to a detailed account of the quarreling of his assistants at Yverdon and a defense against his critics.

STANS

The appointment at Stans seemed to be an opportunity to continue his work with the poor, which he began at Neuhof. Never satisfied with theorization, he was happy to return to actual practice. Not only was the situation at Stans poverty-ridden, it was also devastated by war. The conservative Roman Catholic cantons of Schwytz, Uri, and Unterwalden had refused to swear allegiance to the French-supported Helvetian Republic. A detachment of French soldiers had been dispatched to compel the submission of these rebellious cantons. The French encountered strong opposition and in retaliation burned the city of Stans and massacred the adult inhabitants. The attack devastated much of the region and left many orphaned children in its wake. In order to care for these children the Helvetian government established an orphanage and appointed the fifty-nine-year-old Pestalozzi as director. On January 14, 1799, the first of eighty children was admitted. Pestalozzi was handicapped by limited funds and by the general hostility of the residents who regarded him as a radical and a heretic. In describing his experience at Stans, Pestalozzi later wrote:

> *Alone, destitute of all means of instruction, and of all other assistance, I united in my person the offices of superintendent, paymaster, steward, and sometimes chambermaid, in a half-ruined house. I was surrounded with ignorance, disease, and with every kind of novelty. The number of children rose, by degrees, to eighty: all of different ages; some full of pretensions; others inured to open beggary; and all, with a few solitary exceptions, entirely ignorant.*[17]

Although the situation at Stans was far from promising, Pestalozzi had the advantage of being able to plan the entire program of the school without official interference. The first task was to create an environment conducive to learning. By creating a home atmosphere of love and security Pestalozzi tried to rehabilitate these victims of poverty and war. In employing his general method Pestalozzi sought to create a climate of emotional security. Rather than acting as teacher, Pestalozzi was a father to his household.

Once a semblance of security had been restored to the children's lives, he attempted to employ his education of heart, hands, and head. In giving the instructions in drawing, writing, and physical exercises, Pestalozzi encouraged the children to cooperate with each other and to share their work:

> Since I had no fellow-helpers, I put a capable child between two less capable ones; he embraced them with both arms, he told them what he knew, and they learned to repeat after him what they knew not.[18]

In his work at Stans Pestalozzi utilized the experience that he gained eighteen years earlier at Neuhof. He still retained a belief in the self-activity of the learner. All learning came from innate powers that were stimulated by the environment. He made use of the children's spontaneous self-activity by frequent excursions and nature study. His antagonism to verbal education was evident in that he refused to permit the traditional forms of artificial education to interfere with the paternal relationship between teacher and learner. Pestalozzi revised his conception of preparation for vocational work. Rather than trying to introduce activities to make immediate profits, Pestalozzi now thought the proper mode of vocational preparation lay in the gradual exercise of the child's physical abilities.

Unfortunately Pestalozzi's experiment at Stans ended abruptly when the massing of the opposing Austrian and French armies in the vicinity caused the closing of the school. On June 8, 1799, after only five months of operation, the orphanage was commandeered as a military hospital. Pestalozzi left Stans on the following day. Although the time spent at Stans was short Pestalozzi regarded his work there as a valuable experience. He was once again involved in actual educational practice. He claimed that his experiments at Stans convinced him of the following pedagogical principles: (1) the inadequacy of mere verbalism and the superiority of knowledge based on the apprehension of physical objects; (2) the importance of the child's innate self-activity as a means of developing his moral, intellectual, and physical powers; (3) the efficiency of simultaneous instruction as opposed to the individual recitation.[19]

BURGDORF

In July 1799 the Helvetian government assigned Pestalozzi as a teacher in the common vernacular school at Burgdorf. Intended for the non-burgess or non-citizen class this school was attended by poor children whose parents were industrial or agricultural workers. Pestalozzi was to serve as a teaching assistant to the schoolmaster, Samuel Dysli, who was also a shoemaker. A typical elementary school teacher of the day, Dysli divided his time between cobbling and teaching. The schoolmaster-shoemaker regarded the visionary educational reformer as a threat and soon encouraged parental opposition to Pestalozzi's teaching practices. Although Pestalozzi did not particularly oppose Dysli's combining of work and learning, he disagreed with the shoemaker's traditional teaching practices. In Dysli's school each child learned the lesson that had been assigned by the parents. The main object was memorization of the Heidelberg Catechism, some of the psalms, and selected passages from the Testaments. In addition to memorization of religious materials occasional lessons were given in spelling and reading. Only a few children learned to write or to count. Most of the time was devoted to having the children repeat their lessons aloud to themselves. The children attended school only when they had no work to do at home.

Pestalozzi was given charge of half of Dysli's seventy-three pupils. In place of the individual recitations he substituted simultaneous instructions for the whole class. Since he disapproved of the verbalism of the traditional method, Pestalozzi's charges used no copy books, readers, or catechism. These educational experiments were halted when Dysli succeeded in arousing the parents sufficiently to demand Pestalozzi's dismissal.

After his forced dismissal from the vernacular common school, Pestalozzi's friends secured him a position in a dame school, or reading and spelling school, which was conducted by Miss Stahli. This school enrolled twenty-five boys and girls, who ranged in age from five to eight years. Pestalozzi was allowed much more freedom of instruction with these middle class youngsters than he had been allowed with the working class children in Dysli's school. The children in Stahli's school were also younger and Pestalozzi seemed to have more success with them than he did with the older children. During his work at Miss Stahli's school Pestalozzi began to practice his theory of natural education.

As at Neuhof and Stans Pestalozzi's first effort was to create a love environment. After the general method of

creating a climate of emotional security had been employed, then Pestalozzi turned to the special method of
teaching subjects and skills. While at Burgdorf he
developed his ABC of *Anschauung,* the reduction of instruction into its simplest components:

> *I sought in all ways to bring the beginnings of spelling
> and counting to the greatest simplicity and into form. So
> that the child with the strictest psychological order might
> pass from the first step gradually to the second; and then
> without break, upon the foundation of the perfectly un-
> derstood second step, might go on quickly and safely to
> the third and fourth.*[20]

In teaching spelling Pestalozzi used simultaneous group
instruction. The children began with the shortest words
and then proceeded to longer ones. Movable letters were
used for the first instruction in spelling and reading. In
the teaching of arithmetic Pestalozzi used pebbles and
beans; to teach fractions, apples and cakes would be divided among the children. Only after acquiring complete
familiarity with arithmetical processes were the children
introduced to figures. The initial writing exercises consisted in the drawing of rising and falling strokes and of
open and closed curves. Through these exercises done on
slates the children became facile in the use of their hands
for writing. There were also frequent occasions for physical exercises and play activities.[21]

Pestalozzi made progress in his work in Miss Stahli's
school and succeeded in translating many of his theories
into educational practice. In March 1800 his work in the
school was examined by the School Commission of Burg-

dorf. The commission was impressed with his methods of instruction and reported:

> Whilst by the laborious method hitherto pursued children from five to eight years of age only learn the letters, to spell and read, your pupils have not only accomplished this task with such a degree of perfection as we have not met with before, but the cleverest among them distinguished themselves by their beautiful writing, their talent for drawing and counting. You have succeeded with all in arousing and cultivating the taste for history, natural history, measuring, geography, &c. in such a way that their future masters will see their work incredibly simplified if they are able to take advantage of this preparation.[22]

After so much discouragement the School Commission's favorable report seemed to vindicate Pestalozzi's educational reforms. A group of supporters, organized as The Society of the Friends of Education, raised funds to equip a special Pestalozzian school in the castle at Burgdorf, which would be used as a center for educational research, teacher training, and instructional materials preparation. In 1801 Pestalozzi opened his educational Institute with financial support coming from the Helvetian government and the Society of Friends. The students were composed of a group of pauper children from Appenzell, in eastern Switzerland, and a number of resident children from Burgdorf. It was at Burgdorf that some young men including Herman Krusi, Johannes Niederer, Johannes Buss, and Joseph Neef joined Pestalozzi as teaching assistants. The Institute functioned for three and a half years until federalism was reestablished in Switzerland as a result of Napoleon's Act of Mediation. With the fall of the Helvetian government's authority, the canton of Berne repossessed Burgdorf castle and the Institute was closed for lack of suitable quarters in the area.

YVERDON

After the closing of the Institute at Burgdorf Pestalozzi moved with his teaching assistants to Munchen-Buchsee, which was only three miles from Fellenberg's famous school at Hofwyl. At Munchen-Buchsee, Pestalozzi began a short-lived school that was combined with Fellenberg's Institute, but the two educators were unable to cooperate. On October 28, 1804, Pestalozzi and his followers moved to the old castle of Yverdon, which was given him rent free by the municipality. Formerly a military stronghold, the castle was spacious and contained large halls that were used as assembly rooms, classrooms, and dormitories. It was at Yverdon castle that Pestalozzi attained such great success that the fame of his educational experiments reached all parts of Europe and the United States.

Pestalozzi's efforts were most successful during the first five years of the Institute from 1805 to 1810. Students and interested educators came from most of the European countries. The Prussian government, stimulated by Fichte's *Addresses to the German Nation,* which memorialized Pestalozzi's system of education, sent a delegation of seventeen men to study the method and prepare for its introduction into the Prussian school system. Yverdon became an educational mecca as educators flocked to the Institute to observe the natural method of education first-hand. Friedrich Froebel, founder of the kindergarten, visited and stayed for a brief time as a teaching assistant. Andrew Bell, famous for the monitorial method, came and criticized. Johann Friedrich Herbart, Robert Owen, and others came and observed.

Baron Roger de Guimps, the son of a French refugee who settled in Yverdon, was a student at the Pestalozzian Institute for nine years. His book, *Pestalozzi: His Aim and Work*, provides many insights into the operations of the Institute. The basic curriculum included the fundamental exercises that Pestalozzi called "elementary education," designed to exercise the moral, mental, and physical powers. These exercises, based on the ABC of *Anschauung*, included the study of language, form, and number. Elementary education led to work in geography, natural and physical science, mathematics, drawing, singing, spelling, reading, handicrafts, and gardening. The basic principle underlying the entire curriculum was sense observation.

According to de Guimps, ten hours each day were devoted to lessons. Each lesson lasted for one hour after which the students would change rooms. During the last hour of the day the students were given free time to pursue their own interests. The schedule for an instructional day was as follows:

6 a.m.	First Lesson of the Day
7	Morning Bath and Breakfast of Soup
8	Lessons Resumed
10	Rest Period with a Light Snack of Fruit or Bread

12 noon	Recreation and Games
1 p.m.	Dinner of Soup, Meat, Vegetables
1:30–4:30	Lessons Resumed
4:30–6	Collation, an informal meal, followed by Recreation
6–7	Lessons
7–8	Free Time
8	Supper

When the weather permitted, a part of the afternoon was devoted to military drills, which were usually conducted by Joseph Neef, a teaching assistant who had been a sergeant in the French army. The pupils were formed into a small battalion with a flag, drums, and music. De Guimps claims that they became quite accomplished in performing complicated maneuvers. There were also regular gymnastic exercises; during the winter the students skated and in the summer they were permitted to swim and to mountain climb.[23]

Pestalozzi supervised the entire program of instruction. Three times each week the teaching assistants reported on their conduct and the progress of their pupils. The students themselves appeared before Papa Pestalozzi five times each week. Each child whispered to Pestalozzi who asked them to tell him anything that they wished to about the week's events. Every Saturday the instructional staff discussed the week's work at a general meeting. Although Pestalozzi seemed to keep abreast of the instructional program, once again he was unable to attend to the financial affairs of the Institute, which were always in a sorry state.

During the life of the Institute at Yverdon Pestalozzi attracted a number of teaching assistants who were to make an imprint on European education. Unfortunately

Pestalozzi was unable to maintain harmony among them. The chief protagonists in the conflicting camps of teaching assistants were Johannes Niederer and Joseph Schmid. Their hostility eventually caused the demise of the Institute. Niederer, from the Swiss canton of Appenzell, had been a minister and was well versed in philosophy and theology. He had joined the Pestalozzian group at Burgdorf where he served as the Protestant chaplain and teacher of Scripture. He aided Pestalozzi in his writing and edited parts of *How Gertrude Teaches Her Children.* Versed in Fichte's and Schelling's philosophies, Niederer introduced his own concept of German idealism into Pestalozzi's work. Thus, at times, Pestalozzi's preference for naturalism is obscured by the entry of idealistic language from the pen of Niederer. Nevertheless, Niederer did perform a useful service by struggling to bring Pestalozzi's tangled ideas into a more systematic philosophic structure.

Niederer's rival as successor to Pestalozzi was Joseph Schmid, whom de Guimps described as the "little shepherd from the Tyrol." Claiming that Schmid had "more intelligence than heart," de Guimps said, "He had a keen, crafty spirit, a will of iron, and a hard unfeeling nature." [24] Schmid was a competent mathematician and possessed ability as a financial administrator. Schmid and Niederer were constantly quarreling. Although Schmid once left the Institute he was invited to return and proceeded to introduce stringent economies, which caused Niederer's faction to leave the Institute.

Because of his administrative ineptness and his gentleness, Pestalozzi was forced to witness the destruction of his Institute at Yverdon at the hands of contentious factions of teaching assistants. His basic methodological principle was that effective education required the careful cultivation of a climate of emotional security. In such a home-like environment, genuine education could proceed. Unfortunately, Pestalozzi was unable to maintain the integrity of his Institution and the home-like environment was destroyed by family feuds. A gentle man, Pestalozzi had always permitted his assistants so much freedom that some of his educational concepts were diluted or weakened in the process. Although Papa Pestalozzi tried to be a father figure to his educational household, his gentle but eccentric personality lacked the necessary firmness to bring order to his quarreling associates.

In 1821 a series of charges and countercharges between the municipality of Yverdon and Pestalozzi occurred over the expenses in maintaining the Institute. Pestalozzi and Schmid demanded that the municipal government assume a greater share of the expenses of the faltering Institute. After much anxiety and legal maneuvering the municipality agreed to pay a small sum to defray the Institute's expenses and Pestalozzi agreed to drop his legal suit. These quarrels sapped Pestalozzi's strength and distracted his attention from the educational task of the Institute. Some of the disgruntled assistants then initiated a suit against Schmid, who was brought to court and exiled as an undesirable alien to his native Austria. After nearly twenty years of educational effort, the Pestalozzian Institute of Yverdon came to an end in February 1825 when its founder left to return to spend his last years at Neuhof, the place of his beginning as an educator. He lived for

two years and died on February 17, 1827. In 1846 the
canton of Argovie erected a monument, which bore the
epitaph:

Here lies Heinrich Pestalozzi,
born in Zurich on the 12th day of January, 1746,
died at Brugg on 17th February, 1827.
Saviour of the poor at Neuhof,
Preacher to the people in Leonard and Gertrude,
Father of the Fatherless in Stans,
Founder of the new elementary school at Burgdorf
and Muchenbuchsee,
educator of humanity in Yverdon.
Man, Christian, Citizen.
Everything for others, nothing for himself.
Blessings be on his name.

· NOTES ·

1. Kate Silber, *Pestalozzi: The Man and His Work* (London: Routledge and Kegan Paul, 1960), pp. 4–5.
2. Sister Mary Romana Walch, *Pestalozzi and the Pestalozzian Theory of Education: A Critical Study* (Washington: The Catholic University Press, 1952), pp. 3–4.
3. *Ibid.*, p. 7.
4. Roger de Guimps, *Pestalozzi: His Aim and Work* (Syracuse: Bardeen, 1889), p. 5.
5. Silber, *op. cit.*, p. 8.
6. De Guimps, *op. cit.*, pp. 6–7.
7. Silber, *op. cit.*, p. 13.
8. De Guimps, *op. cit.*, pp. 20–23.
9. *Ibid.*, pp. 24–25.
10. *Ibid.*, p. 29.

11. Pestalozzi, "Views and Experiences," in Lewis F. Anderson, ed., *Pestalozzi* (New York: McGraw-Hill, 1931), p. 100.

12. Karl Justus Blochmann, "Henry Pestalozzi: Touches of a Picture of His Life and Labors," in Henry Barnard, ed., *Pestalozzi and Pestalozzianism* (New York: Brownell, 1862), p. 12.

13. De Guimps, *op. cit.*, pp. 40–41.

14. Johann H. Pestalozzi, *Leonard and Gertrude*, in Barnard, *op. cit.*, p. 527.

15. De Guimps, *op. cit.*, p. 59.

16. Johann H. Pestalozzi, *How Gertrude Teaches Her Children* (Syracuse: Bardeen, 1900), p. 6.

17. Pestalozzi, "Pestalozzi's Account of His Own Educational Experience," in Barnard, *op. cit.*, p. 674.

18. Pestalozzi, *How Gertrude Teaches, op. cit.*, p. 18.

19. *Ibid.*, pp. 17–18.

20. *Ibid.*, p. 23.

21. Silber, *op. cit.*, p. 126.

22. De Guimps, *op. cit.*, p. 102.

23. *Ibid.*, p. 174.

24. *Ibid.*, p. 102.

· III ·
The Pestalozzian World View

Pestalozzi's fame in the history of education has come from the educational reforms that he wrought at the experimental schools of Neuhof, Stans, Burgdorf, and Yverdon. His teaching assistants and a host of foreign observers carried the Pestalozzian theories of education throughout Europe and the Americas. Students of the history of western education are bound to encounter references to *Leonard and Gertrude* and *How Gertrude Teaches Her Children*. Throughout most of the nineteenth and early twentieth centuries, Pestalozzi has been remembered and reinterpreted for his educational theory. Recently, however, a shift of interest has occurred as Pestalozzianism is examined for its philosophical, sociological, and political

aspects. To appreciate the work of Pestalozzi it is necessary to go beyond his work as an educator and to examine
the broad theoretical matrix in which his educational theory rested. Like most of the post-Enlightenment intellectuals Pestalozzi sought to frame a comprehensive view of
the nature of things. This chapter, therefore, undertakes
to examine the Pestalozzian world view.

An examination of Pestalozzi's philosophy is hampered
by his eccentricities as a writer. Logically inconsistent his
writings contained bits of personal reminiscences intermin-
gled with profound philosophical insights. Going to great
lengths to disparage himself as a writer of philosophy,
Pestalozzi claimed that teaching was his source of greatest
happiness. Further, he felt that he could not express
clearly those philosophical concepts that undergirded his
educational theory:

> *My whole manner of life has given me no power, and no*
> *inclination, to strive hastily after bright and clear ideas*
> *on any subject, before, supported by facts, it has a back-*
> *ground in me that has awakened some self-confidence.*
> *Therefore, to my grave I shall remain in a kind of fog*
> *about most of my views. But I must say, if this fog has a*
> *background of various and sufficiently vivid sense-impres-*
> *sions, it is a holy fog for me.*[1]

MAN IN NATURE

As indicated earlier, Pestalozzi shared the intellectual climate of opinion of post-Enlightenment Europe. Like the
philosophes and the later romantics, he looked to nature

as the source of all being. Man's existence could be explained only within the context of naturalism. Pestalozzi sought the natural man. His concept of nature contained all of the eighteenth-century meanings. It embraced the outer physical world as well as man's internal powers. It encompassed the lower animal level of existence as well as the higher human existence. To borrow the terminology of the transcendentalists, nature was the all embracing macrocosm as well as the finite microcosm, which was a small part of the universal being.

Following Newtonian science, nature was a universal mechanism that functioned according to its own intrinsic and ordered design of unchangeable patterns. These universal laws were the same for physical nature and for human nature. As a small part of the macrocosmic world machine human nature conformed to universal laws. Pestalozzi's concept of nature was cast in pre-Darwinian terms, which precluded the possibility of radical transformation or evolution of the basic functional design. Nature was then the metaphysical foundation upon which Pestalozzi erected his philosophy of education.

As a macrocosmic world machine nature exhibited an interrelationship of structure and function. In terms of structure nature is a universal design or plan. All of the parts of the plan share the basic design. Since man can be defined structurally according to his form, his humanity conforms to the basic universal design. Nature is also a functioning process of development or growth. Plants, animals, and men grow according to their structural design. Natural development is continuous and gradual. Each phase must be completed before the ensuing one is

begun. By Pestalozzi's definition man intrinsically possesses moral, intellectual, and physical potentialities. These
defining qualities constitute man's basic structure. Functionally, these powers must be exercised if they are to
grow and reach their destined completion. Human growth
is parallel to natural growth since the same functional
laws are operative. Based on these structural and functional premises, Pestalozzi's philosophical problem was to
discover man's most efficacious means of cooperating with
the natural laws of growth and development.

Structurally and functionally nature is a wholistic, universal totality, which encompasses all existence. In terms
of its structure nature, an architectonic edifice, has a time
and place for all existent beings. In the functioning of the
laws of development its operations are universally applicable. The concept of nature is, then, the highest and
most general category in Pestalozzi's world view. As a totality nature is careless of the individual or the accidental
deviation from the general law:

> *Nature, on whom the inevitable laws of the existence and
> consequences of the accidental are based, seems only de-
> voted to the whole, and is careless of the individual that
> she is affecting externally. On this side she is blind; and
> being blind, she is not the Nature that comes, or can
> come into harmony with the seeing, spiritual, moral na-
> ture of men. On the contrary, it is only spiritual and
> moral nature that is able to bring itself into harmony with
> the physical—and that can, and ought to do so.*[2]

Because man's structure contains moral, intellectual, and
physical potentialities, he is a self-active being. This self-
activity is a motivating force that compels him to act in

certain ways. Although participating in a universal structure of human nature, each man also is uniquely individual because of the accidental and variable conditions of
particular economic, social, political, and cultural environ-
ments. Man's overriding task is to: (1) seek truth in nature and there discover her universal laws; (2) order
environmental particularities so that the accidental may
conform to the universal and general natural principles;
(3) fashion laws of education that correspond to the laws
of natural development.

HUMAN NATURE

Although men might differ as to occupation, nation, religion, custom, law, and society, these variations are merely
accidentally caused by cultural divergences. These acci-
dentals should not be permitted to obscure the fundamental truth that all men, because of their common human
nature, are fundamentally alike. All men are endowed
with the universal and unchanging moral, intellectual, and
physical powers that define them as members of the human race. Based on the constituent powers that comprise
human nature, all men share the same reciprocal right and
duty: (1) each man has the right to develop his essential
powers in conformity with natural law; (2) all men have
the obligation .to permit other men this same freedom of
natural development that they enjoy. The moral society
recognizes this reciprocal right and obligation. Over time,
differences in environmental circumstances developed so
that some men lived in different nations, pursued differ-

ent occupations, and developed unique societal arrangements. These variations were not created by nature but
were, rather, the work of man in society. Therefore, man
has to be viewed from two perspectives: the natural and
the social. Based on these two perspectives Pestalozzi
structured a hierarchy of value that rested on a dualistic
interpretation of man.

Man's natural moral, intellectual, and physical powers
should be cultivated and allowed to develop harmoniously. Social conventions should not be permitted to interfere with this natural course of development. Pestalozzi
maintained that man should always be educated first as
man and second as a particular kind of man. Although he
gave priority to the natural powers of man Pestalozzi did
not neglect man's social side. Social and occupational
differences had to be considered since they were part of
man's existence. Pestalozzi believed that there were certain activities and specific training appropriate to all men.

Pestalozzi's dualistic interpretation of man should not
be construed as a necessary conflict between the natural
order and the social order. Rather these orders were
complementary to man who was a substantial functioning
unity of the psychological and the physical. Walch has
referred to this unity as "psychophysical parallelism." [3]
The harmoniously functioning natural man was a successful blending of the psychological, which for Pestalozzi was
the natural, and the physical, which included man's social
and occupational activities.

THE STATE OF NATURE

The Enlightenment *philosophes* had written about the state of nature, where man's condition was that of complete innocence. Especially for Rousseau, the noble savage in the state of nature was the progenitor of civilized man who was now everywhere enchained by the fetters of artificial social conformity. Pestalozzi, too, entertained an idea of benevolent, simple, natural man. For Pestalozzi, the primitive state of man embraced two stages: the unspoiled period and the spoiled period.[4]

In the unspoiled natural state man was truly a noble innocent who instinctively and harmlessly enjoyed pleasure. In his natural simplicity man was guided by the feelings of an uncorrupted heart. During this stage man was not reflective and satisfied his needs impulsively but without harming others. This idyllic stage of natural innocence was but a brief moment in the history of the human race. As soon as man began to reflect upon his needs, he became selfish and lost his innocence. However, man subconsciously retains the idea of his former state of pure benevolence. Through his innate moral power, man has the potentiality to love and to strive to regain his lost innocence.

Primitive man entered the spoiled stage when he was forced to use reflection and effort to satisfy his desires. The more he plans, the less he can rely on the soundness of his instincts. Soon the plans degenerate into selfish schemes and man becomes corrupted. With the loss of innocence man is forced to construct elaborate means of satisfying his needs and thus society emerges. Natural man is submerged by society with its artificial social and economic distinctions. Acquisition of property becomes a way of satisfying needs. In society men ruthlessly compete against their fellows. The more efficient schemers become the advantaged class and the less efficient are forced into the class of the economically disadvantaged. In the social state men were differentiated occupationally into businessmen, farmers, laborers, ministers, and a host of other specialities. Men were no longer thought of as men but were identified occupationally. Universal natural laws were disregarded as the social order was given preference over the natural order.

For Pestalozzi the social state was not the moral state of benevolent justice, but it was a necessary stage in human development. Because of his innate moral, intellectual, and physical powers, man has the potentiality to develop into an harmoniously integrated individual. Only if men exercise their powers, naturally rather than artificially, will genuine culture be achieved within the moral state. If man makes use of his self-activity to exercise his natural powers, human nature will be restored to pure benevolence. Always stressing the powers of individuals Pestalozzi believed that the social state could be transformed into the moral state by the efforts of individual men.

Pestalozzi's interpretation of man's fall from the state of nature and his projected natural salvation embraced three major phases. In the primitive state man briefly experienced a childlike period during which he instinctively satisfied his needs. For some reason, man could no longer rely on instinct but consciously had to seek to satisfy his needs. This spoiled man's innocence and pushed him into the social state where he became increasingly selfish and acquisitive. In his original state man was benevolent, but this quality had been submerged by selfishness. Man still retained the idea of benevolence. If given the proper educational stimulation, this seed of benevolence could blossom and be the means of man's moral regeneration. If individual men were thus regenerated, then it was possible to restore a community of benevolence, the moral order.

Pestalozzi's account of man's condition since his fall from the natural state had direct implications for the life of each individual man. Like other educators of the period, Pestalozzi accepted the doctrine of cultural recapitulation whereby the life of each man repeated the major cycles of the human race. He identified three phases in human development: the primitive natural state, the social state, and the moral state. Man's growth corresponded to these three stages. Childhood with its basic physical needs corresponded to the state of primitive nature; adolescence with its social stresses corresponded to the social state; the person who achieved genuine maturity was the moral master of his life. The period of natural innocence begins at birth, but is lost with the child's first cry. The psychological distance from the original state increases to the degree that the child's needs are left unsatisfied.[5] The loving care of parents, especially the mother, can lessen the extent to which the idea of benevolence is repressed in the child's subconsciousness. The loving and tender care of the mother will cause the child to respond with love for the parent.

As the child enters the social world the selfish aspect

gains greater control over his personality. The germ of benevolence functions in the child, or in the man in society, to the degree that the individual cooperates with the unfolding of the natural powers. It is possible for all men to achieve the moral state if they can subordinate conformity to social demands to the freedom that lies in their higher powers.

THE POWER OF LOVE

Within the recesses of every man's personality there lies the germinal idea of benevolence. Every child, at birth, is possessed of this spark of the divine. The externalization of this hidden human quality depends upon its stimulation by an appropriate environment. For Pestalozzi, the growth of love depends upon the existence of a love relationship in a climate of emotional security. If a child is given love and care by the mother, the child's latent idea of benevolence will be activated. If he continues to experience tender, loving care, the child will grow into a person who is capable of giving and receiving love. The love relationship is thus a reciprocal one in which love feeds and nourishes love.

If love should be absent in the home circle, the child's needs will be unsatisfied. Frustration will result and the child's germ of benevolence will remain latent. The frustrated, unloved child will grow into the selfish, disintegrated, or emotionally disturbed adult. Pestalozzi's general method of education essentially was based on creating an environment of emotional security.

Pestalozzi was deeply impressed by the mother's crucial

role in the kindling of love. The mother's care for the child activated the latent germ of benevolence into the fullness of love. More helpless than the offspring of any animal, the human infant requires sustained care. The good mother provides this tender, loving care with complete unselfishness. This love relationship between mother and child was a moral relationship in which the mother accepted a set of responsibilities and duties toward the child. Of man's threefold powers, it is the moral power that first functions with regard to the child. The mother's solicitude awakens feelings of gratitude in the child, which eventually develop into obedience to the mother. From this basic set of obligations between mother and child is derived man's moral and religious experience. According to Pestalozzi:

> Obedience and love, gratitude and trust united, develop the first germ of conscience, the first faint shadow of the feeling that it is not right to rage against the loving mother; the first faint shadow of the feeling that the mother is not in the world altogether for his sake; and with it is germinated the feeling that he himself is not in the world for his sake only. The first shadow of duty and right is in the germ.
>
> These are the first principles of moral self-development, which are unfolded by the natural relations between mother and child.[6]

The child who has a secure love relationship with his mother will gradually extend this trust to his father and then to his brothers and sisters. Pestalozzi speaks of the growth of love and its permeation of the entire family circle:

The germs of love, trust, and gratitude soon grow. The child knows his mother's step; he smiles at her shadow. He loves those who are like her; a creature like his mother is a good creature to him. He smiles at his mother's face, at all human faces. . . .[7]

From the security of the family circle the child is gradually introduced to the larger human community. When the secure child encounters other persons he will be ready to respond to them with kindness. The moral principles, duties, and obligations experienced in his particular home environment will be extended to the broader circle of the other members of his family. Of course, the insecure home that lacks love will produce children who will be emotionally handicapped by suspicion and selfishness. These individuals will be incapable of love and because of their selfishness may act immorally. In speaking of the extension of the circles of love from the home to the community, Pestalozzi held that each man's own self-perfection was reached through the perfecting of his brothers. The loving man was thus a humanitarian who practiced brotherly love.[8]

Pestalozzi believed that the mother enkindled religious values in the child in much the same way that she stimulated feelings of morality. Arising from the germ of benevolence moral and religious values were not clearly distinguished but were interpenetrating. The love relationship that was to characterize both the home circle and the community was based upon a humanistic form of religious experience. Although heavily inspired by naturalism Pestalozzi's approach to religious experience resembled the Christian humanism of Comenius rather than the naturalistic religion of Rousseau. As the child grows he becomes increasingly independent. As the child becomes conscious of his powers his reliance on his mother lessens. At this point the mother introduces the child to the concept of God. The following short dialogue from *How Gertrude Teaches Her Children* indicates how the mother broadens the child's moral experience to include the religious experience:

MOTHER: Child there is a God whom thou needest, who taketh thee in His arms when thou needest me no longer, when I can shelter thee no more. There is a God who prepares joy and happiness for thee when I can no more give them thee.[9]

CHILD: I am a child of God; I believed in my mother, her heart showed me God. God is the God of my mother, of my heart and her heart. I know no other God. The God of my brain is a chimaera. I know no other God but the God of my heart. By faith in the God of my heart only I feel a man. The God of my brain is an idol. I ruin myself by worshipping him. The God of my heart is my God. I perfect myself in His love.[10]

Pestalozzi's religion was that of Christian pietism and was a religion of the heart rather than a body of theological doctrine and dogma. Nonliturgical and unritualized, Pestalozzi's religious experience was an emotional feeling of being in the presence of God who revealed himself through his handiwork, nature. Genuine religious experience resulted when man believed that he was directly experiencing God through nature. This true experience of God was unrelated to formal religion which was merely another product of man's social corruption.[11] Self-perfection was man's religious obligation as well as his moral duty. God through nature had given man his natural moral, intellectual, and physical powers. It was every man's duty to bring these powers to completion. Pestalozzi referred to the figure of Christ as the great teacher who through his example taught men how to live properly and how to develop their lives harmoniously. Because of his preference for informal and natural religious experience, Pestalozzi opposed religious education that was predicated on doctrine, dogma, and ritual.

As all theologians and philosophers, Pestalozzi had difficulty in explaining the existence of evil in the universe. The traditional Christian concept of evil has been an absence of good, which is inherited by each man because of Adam's fall from grace. Although the entry of evil into the universe is clearly established by the doctrine of original sin, the origin of evil is not as clearly made. The traditional Christian doctrine of original sin when interpreted by the Calvinist held man to be "depraved" at birth; the Catholic position held him to be "spiritually deprived." Christianity held that man could overcome the effects of sin through the redemptive powers of Christ's grace.

Pestalozzi, like Rousseau, rejected the doctrine of original sin and accepted, instead, the doctrine of innate human benevolence. Since nature is good the products of nature, including man, share in this goodness. The source of corruption is not found in man's nature. Moral deterioration is caused by circumstances that occur in the social rather than in the natural environment. Circumstances of extreme poverty may harden man's heart and make him incapable of loving his children or his neighbors. Social ranks and artificial distinctions may blind man to what is really important in the world, so that he becomes selfish and greedy instead of cooperating with his innate germ of benevolence. In a corrupt society man's interior goodness is attacked from without in the same way that a communicable disease attacks the healthy body. But if man's inner goodness has been strengthened by a loving family and friends, then it is possible to resist corruptive social influences. The course of evil may be reversed by extending the good that lies in the heart of every man. It is possible to reform the social state, to remove artificialities, and to establish the moral state where men and conditions of life are perfect. Pestalozzi's educational theory stressed the cultivation of man's moral sensibilities. Through natural education each man could be so strengthened that he could aid in his own redemption.

Pestalozzi's concept of the innate goodness of man had far-reaching implications for his educational philosophy. His ideas of the nature of man and the problem of evil give strong clues to the modes of classroom organization and the relationship between the teacher and the learner. If the child is deprived or depraved because of his sinful nature, the teacher must rely on external discipline to a greater extent in order to curb the child's tendencies to evil. Once these tendencies are curbed it is possible to relax discipline, but maintaining order is not easy. This attitude toward the child as evil was prevalent in schools during Pestalozzi's day, but he rejected it. Holding that the child was naturally good Pestalozzi believed that this goodness should be stimulated by the teacher through love rather than coercion. In an environment of emotional love and security benevolence would blossom and encompass the whole child. If children were unruly or disorderly in the Pestalozzian classroom, it was due to their upbringing in an emotionally deprived home environment. It was not the child who needed discipline, but the environment that needed ordering.

MAN IN SOCIETY

In the earlier discussion of the state of nature, it was necessary to raise the issue of the social state. It has been indicated that Pestalozzi regarded society as a necessary stage in man's struggle to establish the moral state. Although a visionary and a utopian in many respects, like Rousseau, Pestalozzi was aware of and concerned with the social compact. For a better understanding of the Pestalozzian world view, it is necessary to examine the problem of man in society.

The social state arose when man was no longer able to satisfy his needs in the primitive natural state. In accepting certain group-imposed restrictions each man yields some natural freedom for more adequate satisfaction of physical needs. In society, with its various economic specializations and social stratifications, man's needs become more complex and his obligations are necessarily increased. As the naïve state of primitive equality is destroyed by societal complexity, man becomes aware of the occupational and class inequalities. Life in the social state is a tension-filled existence in which man finds himself torn between the struggle to satisfy the basic physical desires of the primitive natural state and the innate yearning toward self-perfection. Thus man finds himself unable to return to his primitive condition and unable to move ahead to the moral state.

Pestalozzi saw the social state as essentially the same as the primitive state of spoiled nature, with the exception that man must work to fulfill his physical needs. In satisfying his wants each man finds himself pitted against his fellows to gain more physical satisfaction. This struggle is the price of leaving the state of nature. Not only is man in social conflict, but he also loses sight of that which is truly most important—his own self-perfection. To inhibit the social war from becoming violent, men create social institutions, such as government, the church, and the school. They erect social, religious, and ethical codes that are not based on nature, but on perpetuating the social status quo. These conventional institutions and their supporting philosophies rest on social artificialities. Because of its unnatural origin the language that supports the social state takes the form of abstract philosophy, law, and dogma. Education found in the social state becomes highly verbal, abstract, and artificial and adds to man's confused state of anxiety.

Because of the artificiality of the social state the societal structure depends increasingly on symbols, such as property, class, and position, all of which are inadequate substitutes for the natural freedom that man surrendered for physical security. Living in a collective existence requires man to enact provisions and regulations to ensure social harmony. Pestalozzi saw two possible courses that the social state could take: tyranny or civil liberty. If the social state degenerates into tyranny, certain groups seize power and use it to coerce others to do their will and satisfy their needs. Although laws may be enacted by the possessors of power, such laws are unjust and merely perpetuate the status quo. The tyrannical state suppresses the liberty of individuals and violates their natural right of self-perfection. The Napoleonic state served as an example of such tyranny. Although Pestalozzi had once hoped that the French Revolution would move in the direction of increased civil liberties, he later condemned Bonapartism as a form of highly organized tyranny. Napoleon's empire was a collectivistic state that subverted man's natural powers in order to serve the emperor and the power-holding elite.

In contrast to tyranny man is capable of constructing a legal state that guarantees civil liberty to all of its citizens. The legal state, an upward progression from the social state, is a necessary step toward the moral state. Civil liberty guarantees man's physical independence and secures his right to exist as an individual. The legal state is characterized by its just and beneficent laws, its protection of the individual, and its honest and open conduct of public affairs. Such a state, concerned with the welfare of its citizens, paternalistically encourages economy and industry.[12] In such a social environment it is possible for man to aspire to the state of pure benevolence, the moral state.

In the Pestalozzian world view, the moral state is man's highest individual and cooperative aspiration. The culmination of man's striving for perfection is the moral state, a community based upon the reciprocality of love. As the family was an immediate love circle, man in the moral state lives in the context of an enlarged family relationship, the human community. The moral state exists to fulfill man's reason for being, the realization of the individual self-perfection of every man. Man's happiness lies in harmoniously cultivating his natural moral, intellectual, and physical powers. The good state encourages individual self-cultivation, because as a moral community it rests ultimately on moral individuals.

Although various interpreters have correctly designated Pestalozzi as a social reformer, a certain amount of caution must be applied to this interpretation. He was a social reformer in the sense that he believed it possible for man to secure his own regeneration through educational efforts. Always suspicious of any collectivistic approach to social reform, Pestalozzi consistently stressed the individual's role in community redemption. He did not construct any elaborate theories of social reconstructionism, but relied upon natural education as the instrument of both individual and community perfection.

POLITICAL MAN

The problems of political man are intimately related to patterns of social organization. Although some interpreters of Pestalozzi have labeled him as a supporter of the French Revolution, he was not a whole-hearted sympathizer with political rebellion as a means of social and moral regeneration. At the outset of his career he favored enlightened despotism as a form of political organization. Disappointed by unenlightened monarchs he supported the early stages of the French Revolution. When bourgeois liberalism was replaced by Jacobin terrorism, Pestalozzi lost his revolutionary sympathies. Hoping that Napoleon might prove to be a father figure to Europe, he was disappointed by the militaristic imperialism of Bonaparte. When the Congress of Vienna restored peace to Europe Pestalozzi again hoped that the monarchs of the Holy Alliance would rule in the spirit of paternalism. Pestalozzi was disillusioned by the great political figures of Europe as despot, revolutionary, emperor, and monarch alike ignored his theory of natural education.

Pestalozzi himself played a minor role in Swiss politics. He disapproved of the rule of the Swiss cantons by small oligarchies of selfish aristocrats and their upper middle-class allies. As a college student he had taken part in the Helvetian Society and agitated for a reformation of Swiss life. When the Helvetian Republic was proclaimed his support won him educational positions at Stans and Burgdorf. In Swiss politics he supported the Helvetian centralists against the conservative aristocratic federalists. Except for gaining financial support at certain periods of his life, his participation in Swiss politics seemed to have little effect on the formulation of his educational theories. Pestalozzi felt that the particular form of the political constitution had little effect upon the individual citizen. The moral attitudes of individuals were crucial to the good life rather than particular modes of political organization.

In the period before the French Revolution Pestalozzi,

in *Leonard and Gertrude,* emphasized the responsibilities of the aristocracy to provide education and to serve as moral exemplars for the lower classes. In stressing aristocratic paternalism Pestalozzi felt that there was a set of mutual obligations between the upper class and the lower economic classes, especially the peasantry. The good aristocrat was to be a father figure to the peasants and was to protect and care for them. The peasantry, in return, had the obligation to serve as efficiently and faithfully as possible. Pestalozzi's initial attitudes to political authority are indicated clearly as Gertrude tells her children to pray for Squire Arner:

> *Pray every day for Arner, my children, as you pray for your father and me. Arner cares for the welfare of all the country; he cares for your welfare; and if you are good and well-behaved, and industrious, you will be dear to him, as you are dear to me and to your father.*[13]

During the liberal stage of the French Revolution Pestalozzi hoped that the new regime would honor its proclamation of the Rights of Man. As the revolution moved in the direction of control by the lower economic classes, Pestalozzi warned that the masses could be as capable of tyranny as had been the Ancien Regime. The Jacobins were violating man's natural rights to a degree that exceeded the Bourbon oppressions. Although he approved many of the republican aims the revolutionary excesses disheartened him.

Pestalozzi feared that the collective mass was most pernicious to individual freedom. As a true middle class liberal he felt that the Napoleonic empire was most dangerous to man's natural rights. Napoleon had molded collective power into an instrument that repressed man by destroying the independence of the individual. Under Bonaparte the social state degenerated into a tyranny that extended into all spheres of human life. Education and religion were used by this tyranny as instruments of coercion. Even little children were taken by the state and molded into instruments of tyranny.

Pestalozzi was not skilled in the practice of the political arts. Visionary, impractical, and eccentric, political organization and administration were not in his province. It was not unexpected that Pestalozzi's few excursions into politics were unsuccessful. He said that the errors of the politicians prompted him to leave statecraft with the decision to "turn schoolmaster." [14]

ECONOMIC MAN

Throughout his life Pestalozzi was concerned with the plight of the poverty stricken. When he began his educational career at Neuhof Pestalozzi intended to devote himself to the economic and moral rehabilitation of the poor. Admittedly he was the most inept of administrators and as a practical businessman he was a dismal failure. As a theoretician, however, Pestalozzi developed a number of keen insights into the course of economic development. He recognized that the industrial revolution was effecting social change. He further realized that economic change bore heavy implications for education. Pestalozzi was concerned with the effects of the factory system upon the home. In an industrial society the school had to take on more and more functions of the home.

Man's economic relationships rested on the concept of property, which can be most simply defined as those material or physical possessions that satisfy human needs. In the state of unspoiled primitive nature man was effortlessly able to satisfy his needs. There existed in this state the crude economic policy of taking what one needed.

In the social state man is forced to plan and to work to satisfy his needs. As an acquisitive creature man seeks title to those possessions that guarantee the satisfaction of his needs. In the Pestalozzian economic theory, "positive property" refers to the title of possession that men established over the objects that satisfy needs.[15] In the state of primitive nature men had equal access to natural property. In the social state, in contrast, certain men claim certain properties. As a result of the various differences in property ownership, economic differences result among men, thus forming economic classes.

As in the case of the social state man's acquisition of property can lead him in the direction of tyranny or in the direction of morality. If the germ of benevolence lies undeveloped in the individual man, he will be selfish in regard to property. His acquisitiveness can cause him to seek to possess more and more property beyond what satisfies his real needs. Selfish acquisition of property caused most criminal offenses. For example, the villain of *Leonard and Gertrude* is the bailiff-tavern keeper, Hummel, who uses his official position for material gain. He entices the villagers to dissipate their earnings through drinking in his tavern. He uses every means at his disposal to thwart the forces of educational and moral reform led by Gertrude and Squire Arner. Finally, good triumphs over evil as the public exposure of Hummel leads to his dismissal and expulsion from Bonnal. The figure of Hummel illustrates what happens to the social order when the lust for property leads individuals away from nature.

Pestalozzi did not oppose the principle of private ownership but rather sought a just distribution of property that was based upon need. He definitely did not anticipate Marxian economic thought, nor did he seek the abolition of private property. Property was a necessary means to security. Since security contributed to peace the moral state would rest on the security of the right of the individual man to hold property. However, if men were educated according to natural laws, they would come to distinguish their genuine needs from those that were artificially contrived through social conventions. Unhappiness was caused when men desired more than they needed or sought more than they could obtain. Properly educated men would be enabled to estimate their needs in terms of their abilities to satisfy these needs. Such men would need only what was necessary and would seek only that which they could obtain.

In terms of economic life Pestalozzi advocated a doctrine of appropriateness of condition based upon particular occupational requirements. Since occupation was a primary determinant of each individual's membership in a particular socioeconomic class, there were certain needs and a specific vocational education appropriate to particular men. According to Pestalozzi each man should be prepared for his particular vocation. Personal and social instability occurred when children were encouraged to leave the station in life into which they were born by striving to seek higher economic positions. He believed instability to be most common among scholars, theologians, lawyers, and academics whose education was primarily artificial and abstract rather than natural and practical.[16] It should be emphasized, however, that Pestalozzi always insisted upon the subordination of vocational training to the general and harmonious development of the moral, intellectual, and physical powers that were intrinsic to human nature.

Pestalozzi was aware of the impact of industrialization upon the life of the common people. Although preferring agriculture and domestic handicraft he realized that the tides of industrialism could not be ignored. In struggling to live, man was forced to expend effort to satisfy his necessary needs. Effort, in turn, caused man to invent means of efficiently satisfying these needs. The invention of the machine was merely a means of efficiently satisfying physical needs.

The industrial revolution had the effect of moving man farther from the soil and farther from direct contact with nature. Although the natural laws universally and eternally governed human growth and development, the separation of man from the soil caused some men to become alienated from nature. Industrialization also produced an increase of income. The factors of alienation from nature and surplus wealth affected both rich and poor.

Usually the owners of the instruments of industrialization enjoyed their increased wealth to the point that they lost sight of the basic relationship between work and need

satisfaction. Usually victimized by artificial verbal and
abstract educations, the germ of benevolence lay dormant.
Frequently given to the pursuit of unnecessary lux-
uries, such men failed to manifest the paternalism that
was proper in their relations to the working class. Motivated by the pursuit of artificial pleasure, the wealthy factory owners frequently became exploiters rather than fa-
thers to their workers.

Industrialism caused many peasants to desert agriculture for factory work in the city. Uprooted from the soil
the industrial workers were unprepared for their changed
economic life. In his old life as farmer or handicraft pro-
ducer the worker had been able to see the complete relationship between his effort and the production of the crop
or product. Awareness of all the phases necessary in production induced a sense of pride or craftsmanship in the
finished product. In contrast factory work was based on
the routine manipulation of single parts necessary to the
production of the industrial product. The divorce of the
worker's effort from the sense of craftsmanship resulted in
carelessness and boredom on the part of the worker.[17]

The life of the factory worker during the early stages of
industrialism was debilitating. Unaccustomed to the complexity of urban life and the arrangements of industrialism, the factory worker sought to escape his confused
condition by drinking, gambling, and other social vices.
Unprepared for his new role the factory worker did not
know how to use his increased earnings. He wasted his
money on pleasures that caused his own moral dissipation.

Pestalozzi's critique of the impact of industrialization
did not propose that the situation could be cured by a

return to the preindustrial period. Because of a lack of natural education the upper classes lacked a sense of paternalistic responsibility and the lower classes lacked the means of harmoniously adjusting to the changing economic conditions. Pestalozzi proposed a peaceful and gradual means of natural education to enable members of both classes to meet their mutual responsibilities. Industrialism, he felt, could be a means of satisfying man's genuine needs and of reducing poverty. It could be a means of bringing all men to the moral state where each man would accept his responsibilities through a sense of mutual love. He did not suggest class warfare, but relied on the cultivation of the old middle class values of thrift, industry, perseverance, and honesty. If such values were based on love, the industrialized community could also be a love community.

True to the climate of opinion of the post-Enlightenment milieu, Pestalozzi's world view was colored by a predilection for a return to nature. With a Rousseauean distrust of social conventions he believed that man, through his own efforts, could perfect himself through the cultivation of innate moral, intellectual, and physical human powers. Through love, man in harmony with nature could reach the state of moral perfection in an earthly paradise. Although he was variously social, political, and economic, the most important aspect of man was his humaneness, his naturalness. In the cultivation of man's human potentiality education was to exercise a dominant role. In order to enable man to reach self-perfection Pestalozzi struggled to discover these developmental principles of nature upon which could be erected a plan of education. In Chapter

IV Pestalozzi's attempts to articulate such a theory of natural education will be examined.

· NOTES ·

1. Johann H. Pestalozzi, *How Gertrude Teaches Her Children* (Syracuse: Bardeen, 1900), p. 6.
2. *Ibid.*, p. 160.
3. Sister Mary Romana Walch, *Pestalozzi and the Pestalozzian Theory of Education: A Critical Study* (Washington: The Catholic University Press, 1952), p. 81.
4. *Ibid.*, p. 42.
5. *Ibid.*
6. Pestalozzi, *op. cit.*, p. 184.
7. *Ibid.*, p. 183.
8. Kate Silber, *Pestalozzi: The Man and His Work* (London: Routledge and Kegan Paul, 1960), p. 149.
9. Pestalozzi, *op. cit.*, pp. 184–185.
10. *Ibid.*, pp. 194–195.
11. Walch, *op. cit.*, pp. 68–69.
12. Silber, *op. cit.*, p. 94.
13. Johann H. Pestalozzi, *Leonard and Gertrude,* in Henry Barnard, ed., *Pestalozzi and Pestalozzianism* (New York: Brownell, 1862), p. 529.
14. Pestalozzi, *How Gertrude Teaches, op. cit.*, pp. 14–15.
15. Silber, *op. cit.*, p. 61.
16. *Ibid.*, p. 50.
17. *Ibid.*, p. 49.

·IV·
The Theory of Natural Education

Frequently identified with the naturalistic educators Pestalozzi subscribed to the climate of opinion that sought the first principles of life and of education in a return to nature. The naturalism of the late eighteenth and early nineteenth centuries exerted both a romantic and a scientific impact upon Pestalozzi. Familiar with Rousseau's *Emile*, Pestalozzi succumbed to the romantic appeal of the natural man who was unspoiled by the artificialities of a corrupt society. He attacked the excessive verbalism of traditional education and advocated a pedagogical regeneration based on the purity of the child's interests and needs. Like the author of *Emile*, Pestalozzi attempted to popularize his romantic conception of natural education through the novel, *Leonard and Gertrude*.

Although incurably romantic Pestalozzi was also influenced by the currents of Newtonian science. Viewing nature as a precision-like machine the intellectuals of the Enlightenment, the *philosophes*, like their successors believed that the laws of physical science were applicable to society. Using a crude analogy they argued that nature exhibited patterns of regularity, natural laws, which were relevant to man's social life and institutions. A natural society could be based on the foundations of such natural laws. Sharing in this intellectual milieu Pestalozzi sought these natural laws; with the *philosophes* he equated the natural with the good. Embracing Rousseau's romantic idealization of the nature of the child, Pestalozzi accepted Enlightenment science as an instrument that would render the misty world of primeval nature into clear ideas.

Pestalozzi's theory of natural education contained large amounts of romanticism and scientism. While the merger of romance and social science is a fascinating theoretical blending, the interpreter can never be quite sure with which he is dealing. Since Pestalozzi was consistently imprecise in his definition of terms, analysis of Pestalozzi's concepts is difficult. Such basic terms as "nature," "*Anschauung*," "psychology," and "element" were given many and varied usages. While he did not give his readers a well-defined set of analytical instruments, Pestalozzi's life is the story of the educator who was a sometime theorist, practitioner, sociologist, psychologist, novelist, utopian, and agriculturalist, but always a man.

NATURE AND HUMAN NATURE

In relation to natural education nature might be described, most generally, as the totality of man's physical
environment appearing to his senses as a vast array of
seemingly separate, discrete, and independent objects. Following a crude kind of natural realism Pestalozzi believed
that these objects were independent of man's knowledge
of them. However man was capable of knowing them
through sensation and his subsequent reflective organization of sensory data. Although appearing to man as a
misty sea of multitudinous objects, nature in reality was a
highly organized entity that was governed by its own intrinsic set of operations. These operations, or natural laws,
were uniform, universal, unchanging, orderly, and progressive. Although a unity nature must be viewed on two
levels: (1) it is an objective order of reality consisting of a
host of objects, each of which is composed of a physical
content organized according to a structure or form; (2)
nature is greater than these physical objects, one of which
is man; it is a set of operations that brings about the development of these objects. Pestalozzi was concerned with
man's ability to see nature at these two levels of existence,
objectively and operationally.

Holding to a genetic conception of man, Pestalozzi
compared human development to the growth of a tree
from the seed that contained all the innate potentialities
of the fully developed tree. If given a proper environment
the seed develops into a tree. Like the tree, man also pos-

sessed latent, germinal powers for moral, intellectual, and physical growth. As Pestalozzi advised:

> *Man! imitate this action of high Nature, who out of the seed of the largest tree first produces a scarcely perceptible shoot, then, just as imperceptibly, daily and hourly, by gradual stages, unfolds first the beginnings of the stem, then the bough, then the branch, then the extreme twig on which hangs the perishable leaf. Consider carefully this action of great Nature,—how she tends and perfects every single part as it is formed, and joins on every new part to the permanent growth of the old.*[1]

Human nature, a part of great physical nature, is subject to natural laws of growth and development and possesses certain germinal powers, which if given proper environment and nourishment will blossom forth. In further defining human nature Pestalozzi held that: (1) man as a part of nature is subject to its laws; (2) human nature, however, is distinguished from animal nature by virtue of the unique set of intellectual, moral, and physical powers; (3) the development of these powers should follow the natural laws; (4) although developing independently, it is desirable that these powers culminate in an harmonious and integrated personality; (5) although there are accidental variations among men, these differences do not contradict the essential laws of human development.[2]

Pestalozzi, then, held a definition of man based on his unchanging nature as a moral, intellectual, and physical being who, regardless of the accidents of time, place, and culture, remained essentially the same. Man's basic nature was not subject to change although the circumstances of his environmental situation were changeable.

Pestalozzi stressed the concept of the natural environment, a situation conforming to natural laws. His prepared educational environment was constructed upon the unchanging laws of human growth and development.

ART OF INSTRUCTION

Pestalozzi's educational theorizing sought to develop an art of instruction to assist man in growing naturally and harmoniously. Before discussing Pestalozzi's concept of the art of instruction, it is first necessary to justify the need for organized patterns of instruction. If man is a part of nature and subject to natural laws of development, does he then need organized instruction? Would it not be better for him to follow blindly nature's laws?

To Pestalozzi education was necessary to enable man to apprehend reality clearly. Natural phenomena manifested in multitudinous objects appeared to man in a confused way. The art of instruction was a means by which man could form clear concepts from this apparent confusion. The development of man's intellectual, moral, and physical powers required appropriate graduated situations so that growth would be balanced and harmonious rather than one sided. Education was to provide a balanced development within the framework of a prepared environment. For example, the seed of the plant contains the whole plant. The plant will grow, but unless it is given the proper environmental conditions of moisture, light, and warmth, it may develop a tropism that distorts the natural design. The long, spindly plant that struggles for adequate light is actually a deviation from the plant enjoying sufficient light. Man can also experience tropism or environmental distortion that prevents harmonious development. For example, if the intellectual power is overemphasized to the detriment of the moral and physical powers, the particular man may be an amoral, underdeveloped genius. Such one sidedness constitutes a deviation from the natural man. Since harmonious development is preferred it is insufficient to rely on the accidental, chance occasions for growth that might occur in the unstructured environment. In a specially prepared educational environment the powers that distinguish man from lower order animals should be cultivated.[3]

Regarding informal or accidental education as insufficient to achieve harmonious human development, Pestalozzi believed that the art of instruction was necessary for intelligently controlling the growth of man's inherent moral, intellectual, and physical powers. Pestalozzi referred to his attempt to devise a means of intelligent control as the "art" of psychologizing instruction. A crucial shift occurred in Pestalozzi's pedagogical thought: human nature, the natural man, now became the psychological man. Man's thought processes conformed to nature's laws of growth and development. When Pestalozzi describes natural education, he is actually referring to a psychology of education:

> I now sought for laws to which the development of the human mind must, by its very nature, be subject. I knew they must be the same as those of physical Nature, and trusted to find in them a safe clue to a universal psychological method of instruction.[4]

Pestalozzi used the terms "natural education" and "psychology of learning" synonymously. The human mind, like natural phenomena, is constructed to operate according to the laws that bind physical nature. Psychological principles were derived, theoretically, from the observation of natural phenomena. In actual practice, however, Pestalozzi mitigated this view as he worked with children in his various educational experiments at Neuhof, Burgdorf, and Yverdon. In interpreting Pestalozzi, Anderson criticized his inclination to rely on the influence of an extra-human source, external nature, as a source of information about the working of the human mind.[5]

The primary task of developing an adequate art of instruction, or educational methodology, rested upon the accurate identification of man's natural powers. The second phase in methodological construction required a strategically appropriate gradation of exercises, experiences, and materials that could be used procedurally to advance the development of these human powers. According to Pestalozzi:

> All instruction of man is then only the Art of helping Nature to develop in her own way; and this Art rests essentially on the relation and harmony between the impressions received by the child and the exact degree of his developed powers. It is also necessary, in the impressions that are brought to the child by instruction, that there should be sequence, so that beginning and progress should keep pace with the beginning and progress of the powers to be developed in the child. I soon saw that an inquiry into this sequence throughout the whole range of human knowledge, particularly those fundamental points from which the development of the human mind originates,

must be the simple and only way ever to attain and keep satisfactory school and instruction books, of every grade, suitable for our nature and our wants. I saw just as soon, that in making these books, the constituents of instruction must be separated according to the degree of the growing power of the child; and that in all matters of instruction, it is necessary to determine, with the greatest accuracy, which of these constituents is fit for each age of the child, in order, on the one hand, not to hold him back if he is ready, and on the other, not to load him and confuse him with anything for which he is not quite ready.[6]

PSYCHOLOGICAL INTEGRATION

Although instruction was to be reduced to graduated exercises commensurate with the developing moral, intellectual, and physical powers, the product of education, the naturally educated man, was to be an harmoniously balanced individual. All of man's powers were to be cultivated equally so that a balance of intellectual, affective, and physical powers would be maintained or restored.[7] The demand that the educated man be harmoniously integrated is once again based on Pestalozzi's view of external or physical nature. Although physical nature is concretized in natural phenomena, apparently discrete objects, there is an underlying developmental unity, a set of uniformly functioning, unalterable natural laws. In reality external nature is homogeneous and consistent. Human nature, man's psychological structure, likewise is a unified whole, which manifests itself in terms of the threefold intellectual, moral, and physical powers. Pestalozzi warned against rejecting the natural order of education by emphasizing a particular kind of specialized education based on class or vocational differentiation.

ANSCHAUUNG

In his quest to psychologize instruction in order to develop a natural method of education, Pestalozzi became convinced of the existence of a unitary operational process that was the source of all human cognition. Pestalozzi called this process *"Anschauung,"* a multifunctional term. While usually translated as "intuition," *Anschauung* embraced a host of mental activities. Not merely a mental form or faculty, *Anschauung* was the functional process by which man formed concepts or clear ideas. Although Pestalozzi believed his discovery of the *Anschauung* principle to be his greatest contribution to educational theory, his frequent and undifferentiated use of the term has confused many of his interpreters. At various stages in his writing Pestalozzi used the term to refer to every mental operation relevant to concept formation, such as sense impression, observation, contemplation, perception, apperception, and intuition.[8] Because of this imprecise usage, *Anschauung* must be construed as the general cognitive or ideational function of man. Although a vague term it must be regarded as the basis of his learning theory. Curtis and Boultwood comment on *Anschauung* as the fundamental processes of the mind that embrace all and any of the various stages in concept formation:

> *Sometimes it is the process of reception by the mind of a sense impression and the resultant production of an idea*

—an idea of softness, of prickliness, of warmth, of dull-
ness—independent of a knowledge of the appropriate
word used to describe it. Sometimes it is the process of
idea-formation through a combination of sense-impression
and observation—the latter term implying intellectual
awareness or attention. Sometimes it is the immediate
mental realization of an idea without the intervention of
external things. These three versions of Anschauung explain its translation as "sense-impression" or "observation"
or "intuition".[9]

In reference to *Anschauung* Pestalozzi identified five operations for acquiring knowledge, all of which depended
on sensation: (1) accidental sense impressions occurring
during life are sources of knowledge, but such knowledge
is limited by its imprecision; (2) knowledge is acquired by
instruction that has been psychologically arranged according to the art; (3) man may acquire knowledge because of
his desire to know; (4) in the course of his work, man
acquires knowledge; (5) the use of analogy, of compari-
sons and contrasts, is a means of acquiring knowledge.[10]

Pestalozzi's discovery of the *Anschauung* principle led
him to investigate sense impression as the necessary process in the acquisition of knowledge. In seeking to reduce
instruction to its simplest components, an ABC of *Anschauung,* Pestalozzi's methodological quest turned to a
search for the physico-mechanical laws that enabled man's
mind to receive sensory experience and to abstract the essential qualities of sensible objects through processes of
distinguishing, comparing, and classifying. To achieve a
wider and clearer knowledge of the world of natural phenomena, man must be capable of framing and acting
upon more valid judgments. Through *Anschauung* Pesta-

lozzi hoped to give man a rational conception of the world of his experience, which appeared as a sea of confused sensory perceptions.[11]

SENSE IMPRESSION

While not articulating a neatly structured epistemology, Pestalozzi's views on cognition can be analyzed in terms of the three basic phases of sensation, perception, and cognition. Although passive sensation initiated the thought process, thinking, by way of perception, culminated in the active process of framing clear ideas or conceptualization.

Pestalozzi distinguished between crude sensation and the art of sense impression. Unrefined sensation referred to the presence of an external object before man's sensory apparatus in which the qualities of the object impinged upon the senses of smell, taste, sight, feeling, and hearing. Sensation was, then, awareness of the qualities of an object.

The mind receives impressions of the qualities of objects. Always chaotic and confused these sensations are necessary ingredients in the forming of concepts, clear ideas of objects. Through the process of *Anschauung* the mind recognizes the form underlying the diffuse sensory data. Thus the sensations are organized into a structure. Perception, awareness of the object as a structured whole, is based on the contents of sensation and form. Pestalozzi seemed to be using the epistemology of Aristotelian realism in which objects are hylomorphic, composed of matter and form. Sensation referred to the impinging of the material qualities of objects upon man's senses; perception referred to the mind's consciousness of the existence of a form giving structure to these qualities.

The formation of concepts depended upon the validity of the perception. The test of validity was based upon the mind's ability to differentiate between the essential qualities of objects as distinct from the accidental qualities. Essential qualities, necessary conditions, are always found in a particular class of objects; accidental qualities, contingent conditions, are sometimes found in objects. For example, man as a concept always possesses intellectual, moral, and physical powers. Particular men bear certain accidental variations, such as differences of color, size, weight, vocation, nationality. According to Pestalozzi:

> *All things which affect my senses, are means of helping me to form correct opinions, only so far as their phenomena present to my senses their immutable, unchangeable, essential nature, as distinguished from their variable appearance or their external qualities. They are, on the other hand, sources of error and deception so far as their phenomena present to my senses their accidental qualities, rather than their essential characteristics.*[12]

> *By putting together objects, whose essential nature is the same, your insight into their inner truth becomes essentially and universally wider, sharper, and surer. The one-sided, biased impressions made by the qualities of individual objects, as opposed to the impression that their nature should make upon you, becomes weakened. Your mind is protected against being swallowed up by the isolated force of single, separate impressions of qualities, and you are saved from the danger of thoughtlessly confusing the external qualities, with the essential nature of things,*

and from fantastically filling your head with incidental matters to the detriment of clearer insight. It follows, the more a man makes essential, comprehensive, and general views of things his own, the less can limited, one-sided views lead him astray about the nature of his object.[13]

ART OF SENSE IMPRESSION

For Pestalozzi sensation was clearly the basis for acquiring knowledge. Instruction in effective sense impression had to be related to natural laws and to the active process of *Anschauung*. Pestalozzi fashioned a theory of instruction aimed at obtaining clear ideas from the confused mass of chaotic sensations. To proceed from perceptual experience to clear and distinct ideas or concepts necessitated the functioning of numerous mental abilities, such as memory, imagination, thought, understanding, judgment, and reasoning, all encompassed by the term *Anschauung*.

To form clear concepts the child should first be exposed to objects possessing the most essential characteristics of the class to which the objects belong. Such objects were best fitted to impress their essential nature rather than their variable qualities upon the child. Thus the impression of the essential nature of an object overpowered the impression of its qualities. The child learned to subordinate the accidental properties of an object to its essential nature. In conceptualization the following process occurred: (1) the learner recognized the number of objects; (2) he recognized their appearance, form, structure, or outline; (3) the learner named the object by speech.[14] From this description of the art of sense impression arose

the famous Pestalozzian object lesson based upon the
teaching of number, form, and language.

ELEMENTS OF INSTRUCTION

In assessing his own educational contribution Pestalozzi
alleged to have made two fundamental discoveries: recognition of sense impression as the foundation of all knowledge and the reduction of all instruction to three elementary means of language, form, and number.[15] It was upon
these three basic elements that Pestalozzi fashioned his
educational practice.

Although Pestalozzi identified number, form, and language as the elements of instruction, there is confusion
over his use of the term "element." Anderson wrote that
Pestalozzi was influenced by two conceptions current during his age: stages of individual development parallel race
development and human knowledge and skills have developed gradually from the simplest elements.[16] In both
individual and race development there is a building in a
cumulative fashion from the simple to the more complex.
In ordering instruction the origins of the fundamental human powers had to be first identified. An element was a
point of origin from which appropriate exercises could be
devised to develop each of these fundamental powers. Anderson concluded that Pestalozzi's search for natural elements was really a quest to identify the logical, beginning
points of knowledge. The logical based on a system moving from simple to complex was equated with the natural.[17]

According to Brubacher, Pestalozzi erroneously confused the logically simple and the psychologically simple. In going from the simple to the complex the simple element was arrived at by analyzing a subject into its elements. The logically simple may not be psychologically simple for the child.[18] Broudy and Palmer also aver to Pestalozzi's confused use of the term "element." They say that at times Pestalozzi used element to mean both a part of a subject and also a basic mental act.[19]

Silber states that the Pestalozzian elements were not objects or qualities of objects but were the mental acts by which man constructed an intelligible world. But like *Anschauung*, Pestalozzi gave the term a variety of meanings. An element may variously mean: (1) simple, in the sense of the easy as opposed to the difficult; (2) irreducible, in the sense of basic as opposed to complex; (3) the earliest stage as opposed to the more advanced; (4) the natural as opposed to the artificial.[20]

Pestalozzi's identification of an element of instruction was based on his equating the psychological with the natural. He assumed that physical nature followed a set of unalterable laws—one of which was progression from the simple to the complex. The human mind, which was a part of nature and subject to the same laws, also moved from the simple to the complex. His elements of instruction were based on a logical order that assumed the existence of points of origin, developing germinal powers, and cumulative development from the simple to the complex. Pestalozzi sought to reduce instruction to simple acts by analyzing skills and knowledge into parts. Although an element is a mental act or function, such as numbering, measuring, or speaking, these acts were to be exercised according to graduated or graded materials of instruction. The source of confusion in the use of the term "element" came in the preparation of instructional activities and materials that were reduced to their smallest part. For example, the smallest part of a word is a letter. While a letter is simpler than a word in the logical sense, a word is more familiar to a child in the psychological sense, that is, more familiar in terms of experience. Hence the logically simple was not necessarily the psychologically simple.

Although Pestalozzi's three elements of number, form, and language will be discussed in greater detail later in this work, some preliminary discussion is necessary in terms of their relations to the concept of elements of instruction. In the process of making vague sense impressions into clear ideas, Pestalozzi believed man went through the following stages: (1) determining the form and outline of the objects; (2) determining how many objects were present; (3) naming the objects. These stages were related to man's powers of calculation, of forming images, and of making sounds.[21] Therefore the first educational efforts were to be directed to the establishment and development of the skills of numbering, measuring, and speaking rather than to the traditional literary skills of reading and writing.

FROM THE NEAR TO THE FAR

Commentators on the Pestalozzian methodology of instruction invariably refer to the famous dictum that instruction would proceed from the "near and move to the far." In the basic sense this term referred to the literal distance of the perceiver from the object:

> *Strengthen and make clear the impressions of important objects by bringing them nearer to you by the Art, and letting them affect you through different senses. Learn for this purpose the first law of physical mechanism, which makes the relative power of all influences of physical Nature depend on the physical nearness or distance of the object in contact with the senses. Never forget this physical nearness or distance has an immense effect in determining your positive opinions, conduct, duties, or even virtue.*[22]

In a related but broader context from the near to the far meant that instruction should begin with the learner's immediate experience and the objects that were part of the objective conditions of that experience. The progression in experience was to be unbroken. For example, in studying geography begin with the learner's immediate environment before turning to distant regions.

Strong antiverbal bias supported Pestalozzi's admonition to begin instruction with the objects found in immediate experience. Since we come to know reality through sense perception, the nearer our physical distance to the object, the clearer is our perception of the object. If information is introduced verbally rather than directly, then the apprehension of reality is unclear and confused. The experiences of others, as found in textbooks, is an indirect experience not based on immediate sense perception. Like the progressive educators of the twentieth century Pestalozzi believed such information was devitalized and tended to be memorized by the learner without an actual understanding.

From the near to the far also contained a situational implication for vocational education. While believing that all men should be educated generally according to the universal powers found in a common human nature, Pestalozzi also believed that there was a particular kind of vocational education appropriate to specific economic groups. The objective conditions of the environment, the objects in immediate experience, varied according to the particular economic background of the learner. Situations varied according to the different ways in which men earned their livelihood. To begin with the objects in the particular environment implied that a child would receive the appropriate knowledge and skills required for earning a living in particular vocational pursuits.

The principle of going from the near to the far also implied a continuity of experience. While the child's ordinary and immediate surroundings are a means of exercising the powers of number, form, and language, the immediate environment is a part of a larger environment. Ordinarily and naturally the child moves from his nearest surroundings to those that are successively more remote. In moving from the near to the more distant the progress is gradual, slow, and steady so that a continuity is maintained. As the actual environmental continuity is maintained, an experiential continuum is also maintained. Pestalozzi referred to this continuum as the "widening circles of mankind," which led from the home environment through the socioeconomic environment into the total environment.

SIMPLE TO THE COMPLEX

Just as instruction should follow the natural movement from the near to the far, so should it move from the simple to the complex. The Pestalozzian element of instruction obviously points to the gradation of instruction from the simple to the complex. When construed as mental acts or functions, the elements of counting, measuring, and speaking are simple in the sense of being basic to the more intricate and sophisticated arts to which they are necessary foundations. In terms of sound, for example, one would go from the simple to the complex by speaking sounds, then words, then phrases, and finally sentences. Such a progression would extend to the arrangement of instructional materials that would be graded on a logical basis from simple to complex. Going from the simple to the complex might also refer to beginning with a concrete object before developing an abstract principle or generalization.

As all of Pestalozzi's educational theory stresses the maintenance of a continuity of experience, the simple to the complex emphasizes the grading of instructional materials, learning experiences, and activities according to their level of simplicity. Simplicity, again, means logical simplicity in the sense that a part is simpler than the whole. This, of course, does not necessarily mean the easy. Thus a graduated continuum might move from the easy to the more difficult.

Pestalozzi was, then, a sense realist who believed that natural education should be based upon those objects of sensation that were parts of man's environment. Learning

was to be a rigorous kind of sense experience. The Pestalozzian art of instruction was based on the cultivation of
man's power of *Anschauung* and the effective gradation of
instructional materials and efforts on the basis of natural
development. Pestalozzi's struggle to articulate a psychology of learning was only partially successful. His effectiveness as an educational theorist was retarded severely by his
confused and vague use of terminologies. Despite these
weaknesses he did develop a number of insights into
learning theory that would form a permanent part of the
progressive attack upon traditionalism. Among the Pestalozzian contributions to educational theory was his stress
on beginning instruction with the learner's experience, on
using all the educational possibilities found in the environment, and on maintaining a continuum of experience
in organizing instruction. The remaining sections of this
book are devoted to an exploration of Pestalozzi's attempt
to apply this educational theory to the development of the
child's cognitive skills and to the cultivation of a value
structure based on man's natural powers.

· NOTES ·

1. Johann H. Pestalozzi, *How Gertrude Teaches Her Children* (Syracuse: Bardeen, 1900), p. 77.
2. Roger de Guimps, *Pestalozzi: His Aim and Work* (Syracuse: Bardeen, 1889), pp. 246–247.
3. Lewis F. Anderson, ed., *Pestalozzi* (New York: McGraw-
   Hill, 1931), pp. 6–7.
4. Pestalozzi, *op. cit.*, p. 78.

77928

5. Anderson, *op. cit.*, pp. 3–4.

6. Pestalozzi, *op. cit.*, p. 26.

7. Kate Silber, *Pestalozzi: The Man and His Work* (London: Routledge and Kegan Paul, 1960), pp. 139–140.

8. *Ibid.*, p. 138.

9. S. J. Curtis and M. E. A. Boultwood, *A Short History of Educational Ideas* (London: University Tutorial Press, 1953), pp. 340–341.

10. Pestalozzi, *op. cit.*, pp. 114–115.

11. Sister Mary Romana Walch, *Pestalozzi and the Pestalozzian Theory of Education: A Critical Study* (Washington: The Catholic University Press, 1952), p. 101.

12. Pestalozzi, *op. cit.*, p. 80.

13. *Ibid.*, p. 81.

14. *Ibid.*, p. 87.

15. *Ibid.*, p. 139.

16. Anderson, *op. cit.*, pp. 7–8.

17. *Ibid.*

18. John S. Brubacher, *A History of the Problems of Education* (New York: McGraw-Hill, 1966), pp. 210–211.

19. Harry S. Broudy and John R. Palmer, *Exemplars of Teaching Method* (Chicago: Rand McNally, 1965), pp. 110–111.

20. Silber, *op. cit.*, p. 141.

21. Pestalozzi, *op. cit.*, p. 89.

22. *Ibid.*, p. 79.

·V·
Elementary Education: Cognition and Skills

Like all educational reformers Pestalozzi was critical of traditional educational institutions and methods. In *How Gertrude Teaches Her Children* he referred to the crippling of the child's mind, which occurred when natural powers were deadened by unpsychological home and school discipline.[1] After having enjoyed direct experience with nature the child of school age is penned up in an unnatural environment:

> *We leave children, up to their fifth year, in the full enjoyment of nature; we let every impression of nature work upon them; they feel their power; they already know full well the joy of unrestrained liberty and all its charms. The free natural bent which the sensuous happy wild thing*

takes in his development, has in them already taken its most decided direction. And after they have enjoyed this happiness of sensuous life for five whole years, we make all nature around them vanish from before their eyes; tyrannically stop the delightful course of their unrestrained freedom, pen them up like sheep, whole flocks huddled together, in stinking rooms; pitilessly chain them for hours, days, weeks, months, years, to the contemplation of unattractive and monotonous letters (and, contrasted with their former condition), to a maddening course of life.[2]

Although Pestalozzi's description of the formal school romanticized the natural freedom of the child, his description was, unfortunately, all too accurate.

The European pedagogue Diesterweg described the old schools that existed at the time Pestalozzi was seeking to reform education. In these schools, reading, the principle study, was accompanied by the rote memorization of texts, songs, and the Catechism. Since simultaneous instruction was unknown each child came alone before the master's desk and repeated one letter at a time after it was pointed out by the teacher. With the stress on imitation and mechanics children memorized scriptural texts, psalms, and the Catechism. The schoolmaster, usually unprepared for his task, also served in the church as choirmaster and sexton. The children's small tuitions supplemented the salary received from church. Bored by the tediousness of this method the children often became restless. The rod, cane, and rawhide whip, part of the instructional apparatus in each school, were used to force the children to sit still and study their lessons. In addition to corporal punishment other motivational devices were ridicule, kneeling on peas, sitting on the shame bench, standing in the pillory, and wearing a dunce cap.[3]

The humanitarian Pestalozzi found the traditional school to be a pedagogical abomination that brutalized the child and repressed his natural self-activity. Traditional educational materials were based on adult experience rather than the child's interests. The exercises were not ordered in a graduated continuum. Degrading to natural man the traditional school was unscientific and unpsychological. Verbalism had replaced the sense impressionism that Pestalozzi believed basic to the forming of clear ideas.

Pestalozzi thought that traditional European educational methods were based on abstract, verbal, bookish information that was divorced from the child's direct sensory experience. Although believing that books enriched life Pestalozzi did not want bookishness to become a substitute for living. According to his interpretation printing greatly increased the information in higher learning and facilitated the exchange of knowledge throughout Europe. However, while the knowledge explosion occurred in the arts and sciences, the penetration of bookishness into elementary education had destroyed its natural basis. According to Pestalozzi:

> Europe, with its system of popular instruction, was bound to sink into error, or rather the insanity, that really underlay it. It rose on the one hand, to a gigantic height in special arts and sciences, and lost on the other, all foundations of natural teaching for the whole race. No country ever rose so high on the one side, nor sank so low on the other. Like the image of the prophet, it touches the clouds with its golden head of special arts and sciences; but pop-

ular instruction, that should be the foundation of this golden head, is, like the feet of this gigantic image, the most wretched, most fragile, most good for nothing clay. This disproportion, ruinous for the human mind, between the advantages of the upper, and the misery of the lower classes, or rather the beginning-point from which this striking disproportion in the culture of our country dates, is the invention of the art of printing.[4]

Pestalozzi's major attack on the verbalism and bookishness of the traditional school was that it: (1) ignored and weakened sense impression; (2) failed to teach essentials; (3) stressed the isolated teaching of special things; (4) produced letter men, artificially minded logicians; (5) separated theory and action.

By ignoring sense impression traditional education ignored the natural and essential basis for all learning. Only through sense experience with objects could clear concepts result. Since sense impression was ignored the unity of instruction was shattered and the schools tended to stress isolated bits and pieces of information and skills rather than developing man's basic moral, intellectual, and physical powers.

Traditional schooling, based upon mastery of literary symbols, stressed indirect experience through the printed page rather than direct experience. This usually meant that students memorized the literary form of the lesson without necessarily comprehending its meaning. In objecting to the memorization Pestalozzi believed that another person's idea cannot be the student's idea. The memorization of ready-made judgments left man's intellectual power inactive.

Pestalozzi also warned against the "domestic shipwreck," which he held to be common among the learned classes of clergymen, lawyers, and officials who were most exposed to artificial education. These men had been exposed to so-called methods of logic, which gave them a subtle rather than a clear system of rules to govern human thought.[5]

Finally, Pestalozzi was critical of traditional education that made a distinction between theory and action or, in other words, separated thinking and doing. Knowledge, without a sound predisposition to doing, was inadequate. Here again the distinction between artificial and practical knowledge was made. Knowledge that was primarily verbal and that did not lead to the control of man's behavior was idle. Knowledge that led to control and efficiency in practical doing was of real use to man. Using the character of Jost, a visitor to Bonnal, in *Leonard and Gertrude*, Pestalozzi made clear the distinction between artificial knowledge and practical knowledge:

> *Depend upon it, there is a wide difference between knowing and doing. He who is carrying on his business by knowledge alone, had need lest he forget how to act.*
>
> *When a man is in habits of idleness, he is good for nothing . . . the great part of those fellows who have stories out of the Bible, or the newspapers, and new and old pamphlets, constantly in their hands and mouths, are little better than mere idlers. If one wants to talk with them about housekeeping, bringing up children, profit, or business, when they should give one advice how to set about this or that, which is of real use, they stand there like blockheads, and know nothing, and can tell nothing.*[6]

Since the traditional methods of education were unnatural and ungrounded in psychological principles, Pestalozzi sought to structure a new method of instruction based upon natural education. His method embraced the romanticism of Rousseau, a broad humanitarian impulse, and a firm grounding in post-Enlightenment naturalism.

THE METHOD: ELEMENTARY EDUCATION

Pestalozzi referred to his natural art of instruction as the method of elementary education. This meant a methodology of basic or essential education. Most of his work was with children at the elementary level of instruction rather than at the secondary level or in higher education. Although the term "method" was used by Pestalozzi in a unitary way, it encompassed two major phases: the general or broad method and the special method. The broad or general method was necessary to the special method and it is possible to conceive of the special method as a part of the general method.

Pestalozzi was influenced by the Rousseauean romanticization of the nature of the child. This led him to emphasize a great deal of permissiveness so that the child would not be repressed from acting on his natural inclinations. Since nature was good the child's natural impulses were likewise good. These impulses were directed to the developing of the natural moral, intellectual, and physical powers that defined human nature.

Pestalozzi considered himself to be a Christian, but his Christianity was that of a simple Pietism. In regard to the nature of the child, he rejected both the Calvinist conception of child depravity and the Catholic view of child deprivation. According to the traditional conceptions based on the doctrine of original sin, education was to discipline the child and curb his evil inclinations. Pestalozzi, like Rousseau, held to a naturalistic view of child nature, which held the child to be neither depraved nor deprived but to be good. Because of Pestalozzi's acceptance of the doctrine of the child's innate goodness, his general method of education did not stress a form of discipline to overcome any propensity to evil that came from nature.

Rather than being designed to curb the child's natural impulses, Pestalozzi's general method sought to protect the child from social evil, which usually took the form of unnatural artificialities. The child's natural impulses are designed to develop the powers of human nature. In a suitably prepared environment the child can develop these powers.

As well as being a romantic Pestalozzi was also a humanitarian. The Napoleonic wars and the impact of the industrial revolution adversely affected family life and childhood. Pestalozzi's first educational efforts were directed toward the rehabilitation of neglected and orphan children, the culturally deprived of the day. As a humanitarian he wanted to create an environment of emotional security in which the child's natural impulses would be allowed to grow.

GENERAL METHOD: EMOTIONAL SECURITY

Pestalozzi's general method tried to create an educational environment that fostered a climate of emotional security for the child. In other words, the method depended on a love relationship between the teacher and the student. The impulses of love sprang from the innermost being of the child. Like a delicate plant these impulses needed warmth, nourishment, protection, and careful attention. The parents, especially the mother, were responsible for cultivating the love impulse.[7]

For Pestalozzi the reciprocal love relationship between the mother and the child in the family circle was the crucial center of affectional development. The love impulse was so strong in Pestalozzi's theory that it became the source of moral virtue and held implications for social, religious, and aesthetic values. In terms of the principle of going from the near to the far, mother love occupied the circle of human environment most immediate to the infant. In a natural situation the child was given warmth and affection and reciprocated by giving his mother and father gratitude and love. Pestalozzi referred to love as the inner sanctity of human nature, which contained all that leads man to harmonious perfection. Proceeding from a central point of origin the feeling of love regulated, directed, stimulated, and restricted all other emotions.[8]

Pestalozzi's general method was also an all encompassing term in that it included all the techniques, experiences, and forms necessary for intellectual, moral, and physical development. It embraced the entire range of developing man's dispositions and faculties according to the psychological laws of human nature. Pestalozzi's effort to devise a universal method of education was structured on the following working assumptions: (1) since human nature is unchangeable the natural system of education is likewise constant and can be universally applied; (2) every child is capable of developing the moral, intellectual, and physical powers that define him as a man; (3) a natural educational method must provide the sensory stimuli that encourage the development of these powers; (4) since nature develops slowly, gradually, and uniformly, a natural method of education must likewise include graduated learning experiences as a means of securing harmonious development of all the powers of man.[9] These four working assumptions were all interpenetrated by the overriding unification of the love impulse.

Pestalozzi felt that the school should be a specially prepared love environment. While continuous with the home-family circle, it was to extend the familial relationship so that the child would have experience with a larger range of objects and persons. Working in a time of social transition Pestalozzi realized that the family was weakened by the ravages of war and the alterations of the industrial revolution. In cases where the care of the real parents was lacking or deficient, the school had to provide love by creating a climate of emotional security. It should be remembered that Papa Pestalozzi's greatest desire was to educate and to love neglected and orphan children. The various Pestalozzian institutions resembled homes rather than schools.

NARROW SENSE OF METHOD

Although the love relationship pervaded the Pestalozzian experimental schools, these institutions also provided instruction in reading, writing, arithmetic, geography, music, drawing, and nature studies.[10] These various subjects and skills were organized under the three basic elements of number, form, and language. The method of teaching these subjects and skills may be properly labeled as a narrower phase of the Pestalozzian method since it was a smaller part of the whole or general method. For Pestalozzi it was necessary that the general method pervade the total educational environment.

LANGUAGE

Because Pestalozzi believed that each man recapitulates the history of the race, he held that after the real sense impressions of nature, language was the first means of gaining knowledge. He arrived at the principle that the child must learn to talk before learning to read. Language through the power of sound was a means of representing the actual process of making confused sense impressions clear, which then made them unforgettable. Language teaching is a collection of psychological means of expressing impressions and making them lasting and communicable by uniting them to words. According to Pestalozzi:

> *The speech of my race was long only a power of mimicry and of making sounds that imitated the tones of living and lifeless nature. From mimicry and sound-making they came to hieroglyphics and separate words, and for long they gave special objects special names.*
>
> *From this point speech gradually went further. Men first observed the striking differences in the objects that they named. Then they came to name properties; and then to name the differences in the actions and forces of*

> *objects. Much later the art developed of making single words mean much, unity, plurality, size, many or few, form and number, and at last to express clearly all variations and properties of an object, which were produced by changes of time and place, by modifying the form and by joining words together.*[11]

In his desire to reduce all powers to their basic elements Pestalozzi subdivided language instruction into three graduated phases: sound, words, and language. In sound teaching, the child's speech organs were exercised and developed. Instruction in words taught the child to identify single objects with names. In language teaching, the child learned to express himself accurately about the objects he had experienced.

Pestalozzi subdivided the teaching of sounds into spoken sounds and sung sounds. Spoken sounds should reach the child's ear as soon as possible. The method of instruction began with the vowels, then consonants, one after another, from *b* through *z*. These sounds were deeply impressed and made unforgettable by constant repetition. Pestalozzi believed that the simple sounds, such as *ba, ba, ba, da, da, da, ma, ma, ma, la, la, la,* stimulated the child's acuity to sounds. Sung sounds had the additional benefit of adding a dimension of sophistication to tonal qualities and prepared the child for exercises in the singing of complete songs. According to Pestalozzi the teaching of sounds had the advantages of: (1) keeping the child spelling single syllables until gaining sufficient skill to proceed to the next level of words; (2) rendering the repetition of the similar forms pleasant to the child while impressing them on the mind; (3) efficiently enabling the child to pronounce every new word encountered by the adding of new consonants to already familiar syllables. Pestalozzi devoted a great deal of effort to constructing lists of syllables that were to be repeated by the students. It is interesting to note that although he opposed verbal memorization, Pestalozzi favored the constant repetition of long lists of nonsense syllables.

After the sound exercises, the Pestalozzian student proceeded to the next level of language instruction, the learning of words or names. Pestalozzi was being methodologically consistent with two of his stated principles of instruction: (1) all learning derives from sense impressions; (2) instruction should move from the simple to the complex. After a child became conscious of the qualities perceived in an object, he felt a need to name the object. Language was a means of defining objects according to genus and species. Language, however, presupposed psychological maturation in using sounds and the physiological maturation of the speech organs. Both of these latter conditions were satisfied by the prior exercises in sounds.

Name or word teaching consisted of giving long lists of names from all the divisions of nature to the child. The important objects found in nature, history, geography, human occupations, and social relationships were listed and given to the child as reading materials. By making the child aware of comprehensive lists of names Pestalozzi believed that he was facilitating their later instruction in reading and in oral and written communication.

Once again, the name lists were repeated until memorized. As indicated by Broudy and Palmer, Pestalozzi's method contained an instructional paradox. The reduction of materials into their elements was logical in that parts logically precede their complexes. However, this order did not correspond to the time sequence in which the materials entered the child's experience. For example, the child hears the spoken word before hearing the names of the letters.[12] Since the child encounters objects within an environmental or situational context, learning name lists isolated the definition of the object as a name or word from its experiential context. Although a name list is simplified it is even more isolated from continuity with experience than the printed or verbal description that Pestalozzi opposed so vehemently.

The third stage of language instruction, the language lesson proper, combined both the sound and name stages into a more complex operation. Since the purpose of language instruction was to lead men from misty and vague sense impressions to the formulation of clear ideas, language learning was related intimately to conceptualization. The methodological order of the language lesson was: (1) recognition of a particular object as distinct from other objects—as a unity or whole, the particular object received a particular name; (2) the gradual acquisition of familiarity with the object's essential characteristics and their names; (3) acquisition of skill in defining the object's qualities by the use of verbs and adverbs; (4) recognition that situational changes in the object's environment produce accidental qualities that may sometimes be present in the object; (5) appropriate practice so that the learner can distinguish the essential qualities from the contingent, accidental qualities and can describe these situational alterations by altering the words themselves and their arrangement.

Pestalozzi's language lesson was a comprehensive instructional unit that went beyond the spoken word to embrace all of man's funded experience. As a general category, language included geography, history, physical science, and natural science. In so doing, Pestalozzi raised the following questions about language:

> *What does it say of man, regarded as a mere physical being, in relation to the animal kingdom?*
>
> *What does it say of him, as striving upwards through the social state to independence?*
>
> *What does it say of him as struggling upwards, through the forces of his heart, mind, and skill, to a view of himself and his surroundings higher than the animals?* [13]

SCIENCE: PHYSICAL AND NATURAL

As an advocate of naturalism Pestalozzi undoubtedly believed that the natural and physical environment was a rich source of sense impressions. The field trip, a walk through the woods or a mountain climbing excursion, was an integral part of the program of instruction in the Pestalozzian institutes. Children were also assigned garden plots and each child was responsible for growing flowers and vegetables. The environment was regarded as the best teacher of natural and physical science, the study of the plant, animal, and mineral kingdoms.

Pestalozzi believed that every child, regardless of his limited experience, was certain to become familiar with at least six mammals, fishes, insects, amphibians, and worms. In an informal way the children learned the essential characteristics of plants, animals, and insects. They were also encouraged to build personal collections of plants, minerals, and insects.[14] Although the Pestalozzian approach to nature study was one of observing, classifying, and collecting, occasional rudimentary experiments were also performed. For example, snow would be brought into the house and the change to water would be noted.

It is disappointing that Pestalozzi did not fashion a more detailed methodology of nature studies. However there are at least two reasons why the stress in this area was placed on the informal rather than the structured lesson. First, Pestalozzi distrusted verbal descriptions of natural phenomena found in textbooks. He preferred to expose the child directly to nature rather than to reduce nature studies into verbal descriptions. Second, he constructed his method on the basis of the threefold elements of language, form, and number. Nature studies were subsumed formally into the element of language. Informally, however, great freedom was allowed for the child to explore and satisfy his natural curiosity.

GEOGRAPHY AND HISTORY

Pestalozzi included instruction in geography as a part of the instruction in language. Geography primarily was a study of the surface of the earth. From the study of topography and climate, cultural, economic, and political implications were made. For Pestalozzi physical geography began in the study of the earth as formed by nature; it proceeded to a study of the various regional areas and political boundaries; then it led to a consideration of natural resources and their use by the inhabitants of various regional areas; finally, it culminated in mathematical geography, which meant the relations of the planetary system to the wisdom of the Creator of the universe.[15]

Movement from the near to the far was the basic operating principle in the methodology for geographical instruction. Beginning with the immediate environment children explored the local area where they observed familiar places such as a river basin, a forest, or a hill. Then the children drew pictures that indicated the locations of the various places they had observed. In so doing they actually created their own maps. At other times they constructed small scale models based on the area visited during their excursion. The students were taught first to identify the major sites in the area as reference points and then to identify less important sites in relation to the more important. Only after becoming thoroughly familiar with their own locality were the children exposed to the neighboring areas. In such a way the child was led from the near to the far, or from the immediate vicinity of the school, to the neighborhood, to the district, to the canton, to the country, and then to larger geographical entities, such as continents and oceans. The field trip serving as a geography lesson also was a nature study excursion, in that topography was studied along with the plant and animal life of the area.

Pestalozzi was reluctant to include historical studies in the elementary curriculum. He felt that history had become primarily a verbal exercise that tried to impress facts, causes, and effects on children at an age when they were unable to execute correct judgments on such abstract matters.[16] History could also dull the moral sensitivity of children by exposing them to knowledge of wickedness and atrocities before they were able to understand that such unfortunate occurrences resulted from human error. Pestalozzi generally believed that historical studies should not be introduced too early since they interfered with continuity in the child's experience. Therefore the Pestalozzian method restricted historical instruction to lists of major persons and events that might be useful at a later stage of development.

FORM

Form was the second basic means of elementary instruction. As a natural realist Pestalozzi held that the objects that impinge upon man's senses have both a physical content and a structural design or form. The exercises in form were meant to isolate the form from the content and to arrive at conceptualization or clear ideas. Seeking to reduce instruction to basic elements Pestalozzi subdivided instruction in form into the art of measuring, the art of drawing, and the art of writing.

As in all other learning the art of measurement was based on sense experience. As a result of sense experience the student became conscious that the material component of all objects is organized according to some kind of design or form. This simple awareness of form, arrived at through unrefined sense experience, was a necessary but inadequate source of accurate concepts. In order to facilitate the making of accurate judgments as to proportion, Pestalozzi devised the ABC of Form, which he sometimes called his greatest pedagogical contribution. This ABC of Form or intuitional alphabet was based on an arrangement of a series of geometrical forms designed to exercise the child's measuring ability. The basis of this alphabet was a symmetrical subdivision of a square into a number of fixed geometrical forms, such as the horizontal and perpendicular rectangles, the circle, semicircle, quarter-circle, and various ovals. According to Pestalozzi:

> *Thus in order to found the art of drawing, we must subordinate it to the art of measuring, and endeavour to organize as definite measuring forms the divisions into angles and arcs that come out of the fundamental form of the square, as well as its rectilinear divisions.*
>
> *This ABC of Form (ABC of Anschauung), however, is an equal division of the square into definite measureforms, and requires an exact knowledge of its foundations —the straight line into a vertical or horizontal position.*
>
> *These divisions of the square by straight lines produce certain forms for defining and measuring all angles, as well as the circle and all arcs. I call the whole the ABC of Anschauung.*[17]

Pestalozzi's ABC of Form was designed to teach the child to recognize geometrical forms and to copy and use them. Measuring was to develop a sense of proportion by which the child could express himself clearly regarding the relationships of height and width. After becoming facile in measuring, the child was ready to begin the exercises in the art of drawing, which was a linear definition of forms whose shape and content had already been correctly established by accurate measurement. The drawing exercises were designed to exercise the ability to represent correctly the outlines of any object after merely looking at it. Drawing began with the straight line, the simplest element of form. The student first drew horizontal lines, then vertical lines, and then right angles. After becoming familiar with these basic lines he then proceeded to the drawing of figures that used these lines.

Before beginning the writing exercises Pestalozzi insisted that the drawing exercises be completed. In cases where children learned to write before learning to draw, the skill in drawing was spoiled. Pestalozzi believed that writing too early produced a rigidity in the flexibility needed to draw. Practice in drawing also made the formation of letters easier. In other words, he stressed a readiness for writing that could be developed only by the two preceding gradual steps, measuring and drawing. Pestalozzi then divided writing into two stages: the gaining of familiarity with the forms of letters and their combinations, independently of the use of the pen; practice in the use of the pen, the proper writing instrument.

During the first stage in the art of writing the child used a writing book in which the letters correctly appeared. The child studied the forms of the letters and practiced them on a slate. Gradually he proceeded from the simple forms of the letters to the complex and then to combinations of several letters. He progressed to the writing of words that contained only those letters he was able to make perfectly. Once the child, by repetition, was able to write his letters perfectly on a slate, then he did the exercises with a pen.

Pestalozzi recommended that the writing exercises be integrated with the language lessons. Such a combination confirmed the grammatical skill that the child already possessed. The word lists forming the basis of the name lessons were used as spelling lists. After practice in writing the learner compiled his own list of words or his own dictionary.

NUMBER

Although sound and form led by several subordinate methods to concept formation, arithmetic, the only method unconnected with subordinate means, aimed most directly at clear ideas, the goal of all instruction. Although sound and form frequently deceived, number was never deceptive. It alone led to certain results. Measurement's claim to accuracy rested on its use in conjuction with arithmetic. Through use of arithmetic man became clearly conscious of the relations of more or less in all sensible objects and was enabled to represent these ratios accurately. According to Pestalozzi arithmetic arose from the putting together and separating of units:

> Its basis, as I said, is essentially this. One and one are two, and one from two leaves one. Any number, whatever it may be, is only an abbreviation of this natural, original method of counting.[18]

In the teaching of number Pestalozzi again stressed the methodological primacy of sense impression. Instruction was never to begin with the abstract mathematical principles and tables that were usually memorized by students in conventional schools, but was always to begin with concrete objects. The consciousness of many or few was produced by placing real, movable objects before the child. The first number exercises, related to man's germinal capacity for counting, were based on grouping, separating, and comparing objects. In working with real objects Pestalozzi held counting to be an exercise of man's reason and not mere memory or routine work. After gaining facility in counting of real objects the child was exposed to the counting tables where the sequences of relationships were indicated by series of strokes and dots.

Pestalozzi began his number teaching by giving the students the conceptions of numbers from one to ten, first with the help of actual objects and then later by lines and dots on tables. Only when the children had been thoroughly exercised in the counting of objects, such as peas and pebbles, did the instruction proceed to figures, which were regarded as abbreviations of the specific relations of more or less that had been developed by the counting exercises.

To facilitate division, multiplication, and understanding of fractions, Pestalozzi devised his table of units based on the square. He believed that the square lent itself to simple visual subdivision and partition. In commenting upon Pestalozzi's use of the square, Pinloche said:

> . . . it was necessary to find a figure capable of being divided into an infinite number of parts, similar to the whole and to one another, a figure by which fractions gained by division may be brought into the child's perception in such a manner that every relation of a fraction

*to the whole may stand as clear and distinct before the
child's eyes, as the number one is in the child's eyes dis-
tinctly contained three times in the number three.*[19]

Through the use of the square Pestalozzi combined his
ABC of Form with his ABC of Number. Through the
harmony of form and number geometrical figures became
necessary elements in teaching the relations of number.
The relations of numbers became the first elements in
teaching measuring.

SIMULTANEOUS INSTRUCTION

Before concluding this chapter on the method of elementary education, some comments are appropriate on Pestalozzi's discovery of simultaneous instruction and on his
view of the role of the teacher. It may be recalled that in
traditional recitation the teacher called children individu-
ally to his desk. Here the child recited his lesson, which
had been memorized previously, according to the catechetical method of definite questions and answers.

While at Stans Pestalozzi was charged with the teaching of many children without the aid of an assistant. In
order to deal with large numbers of children he devised
the method of simultaneously instructing the entire class.
The learners were to read, draw, and work together. In
describing his use of the principle at Stans Pestalozzi
said:

*As I was obliged to give the children instruction, alone,
and without help, I learned the art of teaching many to-*

*gether; and since I had no other means but loud speaking,
the idea of making the learners draw, write, and work at
the same time, was naturally developed.*[20]

*If many children are taught together, the emulation
aroused and the reciprocal imparting to one another of
what has been gained becomes more easy among the children themselves, and the hitherto round about ways of
enriching the memory may be avoided or shortened by
other arts, e.g. by analogy of subjects, discipline, increased
attention, loud repetition, and other exercises.*[21]

The use of simultaneous group instruction also confirmed
Pestalozzi's theoretical premise of moving from the simple to the complex. Since he was dealing with a heteroge-
neous group of students Pestalozzi was compelled to spend
considerable time on the basic skills. Mastery of the instructional elements contributed to later, more complicated
lessons. Simultaneous instruction also necessitated prior
lesson planning by the teacher who had to organize and
graduate his lessons in such a way that instruction was
orderly and gradual. A methodology of instruction geared
to group situations also occasioned questions of socialization and intergroup relationships. Pestalozzi felt that simultaneous instruction was beneficial in that it saved time
and produced situations in which the children could imitate each other so that instruction was reciprocally im-
parted from child to child. As his theory was put into educational practice, Pestalozzi remarked:

*The utter ignorance of all made me stay long over the
beginnings; and this led me to realize the high degree of
inner power to be obtained by perfecting the first begin-*

nings, and the result of a feeling of completeness and perfection in the lowest stage. I learned, as never before, the relation of the first steps in every kind of knowledge to its complete outline; and I felt, as never before, the immeasurable gaps, that would bear witness in every succeeding stage of knowledge, to confusion and want of perfection on these points.[22]

THE TEACHER

The development of any educational methodology has necessary implications for the teacher. Like Comenius, Pestalozzi believed that a science of instruction would lighten the teacher's task and, at the same time, make learning proceed more efficiently. The method itself became the primary ingredient in successful education as the suitably trained teacher complemented the method. Although methodological competence was required for efficient instruction, Pestalozzi also emphasized that the successful teacher needed an appropriate personality for dealing with children. In *Christopher and Elizabeth* Pestalozzi contrasted the "open-hearted" teacher with the narrow pedant:

> But if the children must need be sent to school, the schoolmaster should, at least, be an open-hearted cheerful, affectionate, and kind man, who would be as a father to the children; a man made on purpose to open children's hearts, and their mouths, and to draw forth their understandings, as it were, from the hindermost corner. In most schools, however, it is just the contrary; the school master seems as if he were made on purpose to

shut up children's mouths and hearts, and to bury their
good understandings ever so deep under ground. That is
the reason why healthy and cheerful children, whose
hearts are full of joy and gladness, hardly ever like school.
Those that show best at school are the children of whin-
ing hypocrites, or of conceited parish-officers; stupid
dunces, who have no pleasure with other children.[23]

The successful schoolmaster's personality complemented
Pestalozzi's broad method, the cultivation of an environment of emotional security. In the home circle the child's
natural impulses to love were awakened by parental love.
In the school the loving teacher cooperated with these dispositions to love by structuring the method for teaching
subjects and skills within the broad context of emotional
security. If the teacher was incapable of giving and receiving love, then instruction in the special methods of sound,
form, and number would be ineffective. The requirements for success in teaching were a loving disposition
and skill in educational psychology.

In the Pestalozzian school the motivation to learn was
grounded in the love relationship between teacher and
student rather than in the learner's fear of the teacher.
Love for the child would kindle love in the child; after
love came the sense of duty and obligation.[24] Discipline
arose from the love relationship. In the rare cases where
punishment was necessary it was to be applied calmly and
with a parent-like concern for the welfare of the child.
The teacher was to separate punishment from the learning task so that the child would not connect punishment
with learning and thereby fear learning. Pestalozzi related
many problems of discipline to the teachers' inability to

motivate their pupils. Children, he felt, should not be punished for the methodological deficiencies of teachers. Pestalozzi also disapproved of the intrusion of external motivation in the form of rewards, incentives, and competition into the learning situation. Genuine motivation was intrinsic and arose from the child's actual use of his own powers.

Teachers who were emotionally secure themselves could employ the special methods of instruction in language, form, and number. They could carry out the methodological implications of making instruction conform to the natural principles of moving from the near to the far, from the simple to the complex, and from the particular to the general. According to Pestalozzi, the principles of natural education were a pedagogical necessity:

> This is essential. I believe it is not possible for common popular instruction to advance a step, so long as formulas of instruction are not found which make the teacher, at least in the elementary stages of knowledge, merely the mechanical tool of a method, the result of which springs from the nature of the formulas and not from the skill of the man who uses it.[25]

In the place of traditional verbal education Pestalozzi sought to effect an educational reformation based on the laws of nature. He gave methodological primacy to the cultivation of emotional security in the learner. Once the child loved the teacher instruction in the basic elements of language, form, and number could take place. Having its origin in sense impression such instruction followed the course of natural development. All instruction, accordingly, began with the learner's experience and moved from the near to the far, from the simple to the complex, and from the particular to the general. The good teacher was the good-hearted person who loved children and who followed these natural principles. Pestalozzi's elaboration of the cognitive dimension of natural education did not exclude considerations of value. The following chapter is concerned with his efforts to propound an educational theory that would enable men to follow their natural disposition to goodness.

· NOTES ·

1. Johann H. Pestalozzi, *How Gertrude Teaches Her Children* (Syracuse: Bardeen, 1900), p. 18.
2. *Ibid.*, p. 28.
3. A. H. Diesterweg, "Account of Old Schools," in Henry Barnard, ed., *Pestalozzi and Pestalozzianism* (New York: Brownell, 1862), pp. 16–17.
4. Pestalozzi, *op. cit.*, p. 140.
5. Roger de Guimps, *Pestalozzi: His Aim and Work* (Syracuse: Bardeen, 1889), p. 254.
6. Johann H. Pestalozzi, *Leonard and Gertrude*, in Barnard, *op. cit.*, pp. 592–593.
7. Johann H. Pestalozzi, "Views and Experiences," in Lewis F. Anderson, ed., *Pestalozzi* (New York: McGraw-Hill, 1931), p. 120.
8. *Ibid.*, p. 114.
9. Sister Mary Romana Walch, *Pestalozzi and the Pestalozzian Theory of Education: A Critical Study* (Washington: The Catholic University Press, 1952), pp. 118–120.
10. Harry S. Broudy and John R. Palmer, *Exemplars of*

Teaching Method (Chicago: Rand McNally, 1965), pp. 109–110.

11. Pestalozzi, *How Gertrude Teaches, op. cit.*, p. 150.
12. Broudy and Palmer, *op. cit.*, p. 114.
13. Pestalozzi, *How Gertrude Teaches, op. cit.*, p. 102.
14. Walch, *op. cit.*, pp. 130–132.
15. *Ibid.*, pp. 127–128.
16. *Ibid.*, pp. 128–129.
17. Pestalozzi, *How Gertrude Teaches, op. cit.*, pp. 118–119.
18. *Ibid.*, p. 133.
19. A. Pinloche, *Pestalozzi and the Foundation of the Modern Elementary School* (New York: Scribner, 1901), p. 253.
20. Pestalozzi, *How Gertrude Teaches, op. cit.*, pp. 16–17.
21. *Ibid.*, pp. 41–42.
22. *Ibid.*, p. 17.
23. Pestalozzi, *Christopher and Alice*, in Barnard, *op. cit.*, p. 667.
24. Broudy and Palmer, *op. cit.*, p. 108.
25. Pestalozzi, *How Gertrude Teaches, op. cit.*, p. 41.

·VI·
Attitudinal Dimension: Heart, Head, Hands

Pestalozzi's attempts to articulate a natural method of education based upon the elements of sound, form, and number were related primarily to cognition, the process of forming clear concepts from confused sense impressions. In his educational theorizing he failed to distinguish clearly between the cognitive and the attitudinal dimensions of education. For purposes of analysis, however, it is convenient to discuss Pestalozzi's views of harmonious moral, intellectual, and physical development from an axiological perspective. His epistemology and axiology were interpenetrating since the principles of natural growth were prescriptive of harmonious development.

HARMONIOUS DEVELOPMENT

The model of the educated man that Pestalozzi preferred was contained in his statement, "He was such a man as all should be." [1] The naturally educated man was characterized by the harmonious development of all his human powers and capacities. Education served to elaborate those qualities that defined and elevated man from the animal level. Since education for harmonious development integrated and balanced man's essential moral, intellectual, and physical powers, the preferred model of the educated man was of good heart, of discerning mind, and fitted to work in his particular station in life.

To be of good heart meant that the Pestalozzian model of man was a person who was emotionally secure in the sense of being capable of loving others and of receiving their love in reciprocation. The good-hearted man because of his capacity to love and care for others was a person who was aware of his moral duties and responsibilities.

To be of discerning mind meant that the preferred model of the educated man was a product of natural education. Rejecting artificialities the discerning man trusted his senses and sought to train them as his most accurate means of seeing reality clearly. Through an education based on language, form, and number, the Pestalozzian natural man exercised and developed his intellect. Finally, the educated man was physically developed to the point that he was an economically self-sufficient individual.

Although exhibiting moral, intellectual, and physical

propensities, the Pestalozzian natural man was not one-
sidedly developed but was an integrated person. As Pestalozzi remarked, "Man is an independent whole and is of
value in himself and in his community only in so far as in
all his relationships he is what he should be." [2] He was
concerned with the development of man's human powers
as man rather than as a specialist. This general power
came from achieving an integrated balance that blended
the powers of feeling, thinking, and acting into an inner
unity. The realization of this general human power culminated in the mature personality fitted for the moral state.

Only concerted effort could achieve this moral, intellectual, and physical harmony. Ultimately, however, Pestalozzi relied on what he believed was the primary human
motive force, love. As the essential means of unfolding
man's general potentiality for self-realization, love existed
innately in every man. However man needed instruction
to fashion his needs into priorities that permitted him to
develop his humanness. True love and faith were attain-
able only in the context of truth based on a clear vision of
reality. Man's values and preferences depended on his apprehension of reality. Man's intellectual education, awareness of reality, in turn was related to the practical areas of
earning a livelihood. Thus a close interpenetration of the
moral, mental, and practical was necessary to achieve the
balanced and integrated Pestalozzian vision of the natural
man.[3]

HOME CIRCLE——MOTHER LOVE

Before turning to a more detailed discussion of each of the essential human powers, it is appropriate to examine man's relationships in the home circle of environment where the correct preferential dispositions were born and nourished. The first values arose as the child interacted with and responded to the mother's love. From the home circle the child eventually moved out to those broader relationships that characterized his social and occupational circle and eventually reached the universal or total environment. In this moving from the near to the far Pestalozzi used the same principle for value education that he did for instruction in cognition and skill.

Well aware of the effects of early environmental experience upon the child, Pestalozzi identified the home circle of the family as the child's point of departure into the larger world of experience. In the home value preferences, emotional dispositions, were fostered. Since education begins at birth the home was the most powerful influence upon the moral, intellectual, and physical development of the child. In the home and from the family the child learned the human incentives, motives, and needs that would characterize his later personality structure.

Since Pestalozzi grounded his theory of human growth and development in man's capacity for love, the good home was one in which all family members shared the love bond. If parents loved each other and loved their children this expansive love relationship would enkindle more love. According to Pestalozzi:

> *It is unconditionally true; where love and the ability to love are found in the home circle there one can confidently predict that the education it affords almost never fails.*[4]

Pestalozzi's general method of education was directed to the restoration and the cultivation of a climate of emotional security. He believed the work of instruction was much advanced where students came from a loving home environment. Children lacking in good will, vigor, and activity had been victimized by parents who failed to give the child's love and lovability that nourishment and direction needed for further growth. The ideal home situation, based on the love relationship, integrated the moral, intellectual, and physical values.

Pestalozzi's concept of the ideal family was typified in the home of Leonard and Gertrude. The major figure in this family was Gertrude who personified the ideal loving mother. The Pestalozzian mother figure positioned in the inner circle satisfied the personal needs of the family members. Woman's nature is the great civilizing influence that was to show mankind the way to salvation.[5] The mother introduced the child to nature and taught him to recognize objects. It was Gertrude who taught her children reading, writing, arithmetic, spinning, housekeeping, orderliness, cleanliness, honesty, and morality. In the home moral, intellectual, and practical education had their source.[6]

The mother figure was particularly important in Pestalozzi's educational theory since maternal love awakened within the child the germ of love. Because of the maternal instinct the mother satisfied the needs of the child for food, warmth, and affection. The child responded to the loving care of the mother with gratitude, a kind of love payment. The mother felt a duty to care for the child; the child, in turn, responded and experienced a sense of obligation to obey. In this rudimentary experience of mutual and reciprocal obligations were born the seeds of the more complex moral and social obligations that characterized the child's later life as an adult.

The home circle was the foundation of Pestalozzi's natural plan of education. Since the development of values in childhood were the securest foundations of the integrated personality, the education that aimed for wholesome family life took precedence over definite occupational training or preparation for a particular social rank. The home and family relationships provided the means by which the child would move to the larger environmental circle of social relationships.

Although believing that genuinely natural education must take place in a homelike environment, Pestalozzi feared that the effectiveness of home education was failing to keep pace with social changes wrought by industrialization. The greater the pace of social change, the more difficult it was for the home to satisfy the child's educational needs. For example, the factory system had removed the instruments for earning a living from the home. Spinning wheels were replaced by textile looms located in the factory. As city populations increased, the garden plot associated with country life disappeared. Children no longer participated in the family's work. Another disruptive effect of the early industrial revolution was the tendency to separate the family members as an effective socioeconomic unit. The father, the mother, and the children might all work in separate shops and factories and be together only for eating and sleeping. Although the homelike environment was necessary for education it was becoming increasingly evident that the school had to take on more and more of the educational functions of the home. In pointing to the need for schools, Pestalozzi said:

> In order to compensate for these almost unavoidable lim-
> itations of home education schools were established. Their
> aim was to make good the deficiencies of home educa-
> tion and to fill out the gap between the limited possibili-
> ties of home life and the steadily increasing demands of
> society and to this end to bring within reach of all the
> culture possessions of the race.[7]

Aware of the close educational relationships between home and school, Pestalozzi stressed the immense importance of the family circle upon the child's first emotional experience. He believed the school to be part of an educational continuum that carried the child forward into the larger circles of experience. Both home and school were essential parts of the continuum and each institution influenced the other. In harmony with the home the school was to continue, expand, and complete the growth of the powers and capacities that developed originally in the home. Thus the home circle, especially the mother, was of crucial significance in developing man's powers into a desired value pattern.

MORAL VALUES

Moral values arose in the context of the family circle of love relationships. From this context came the moral imperatives of obligation and duty. The child learned habits of love and duty prior to thinking and acting. According to Pestalozzi moral values were responses to the love relationship. Developmentally prior to intellectual and physical values the moral values guided the direction of thought and action. Simply put, the man who is good of heart will necessarily think good thoughts and perform good deeds.

In terms of moral education the Pestalozzian plan relied on the *Anschauung* principle, which rendered obscure sense impressions into clear ideas. In saying that life teaches, Pestalozzi indicated that feelings of morality were a natural outgrowth of man's innate capacity for love. If given the proper climate of emotional security these feelings would blossom in the good-hearted man. The educator's task was to preserve these virtuous feelings and habits by providing experiences where these dispositions could be satisfied. Habituation to goodness was to be based on real experience rather than on verbal prescriptions, homilies, and sermons. In other words, morality was felt rather than talked about.

RELIGIOUS VALUES

Pestalozzi's own religious values were based on humanitarian Christian piety rather than adherence to any particular doctrinal, dogmatic, or ritualistic denominational persuasion. His Christianity regarded Christ as a love figure who loved each man for his own sake and who in turn should be loved by all. Like Comenius he regarded Christ as the great teacher and exemplar for men. If Pestalozzi must be identified religiously he was a kind of pietistical Protestant who practiced a religion of the heart without needing a rigorously formulated theology.

It is difficult to isolate the Pestalozzian religious values from the broader context of morality from which they were derived and of which they were a part. The humanitarian impulse was basic to religious values in that man had first to love his fellow man before he could love God. The feelings of love, trust, gratitude, and obedience had to be developed in each individual man before being applied to God. Religious values developed in the same home circle as did moral values. The mother's love for the child effected in the child a loving response that was extended first to the mother, then to other members of the family, to individuals outside of the family circle, and then to God as the Father of all men. In cultivating moral-religious values the basic Pestalozzian methodology operated as the movement from the immediate family circle to the broader social environment—from the near to the far. In loving his mother, father, and brothers and sisters, then other individuals, and finally God, the child was beginning with the particular and tending to the more abstract and most general.

In terms of its educational role Pestalozzi conceived of the church as a cooperating and encouraging institution rather than as a teaching agency. The true work of the church was to promote actively a higher, better, and hence more natural life on earth by serving to crystallize and portray the human condition in terms of a reciprocal love relationship between man and God. Based upon his conception of God as universal Father, Pestalozzi felt that the church's function was to promote those values and qualities that aided man to achieve perfection. When engaged in theological disputation and doctrinal debate the church failed to aid in the important task of humanizing man.

Pestalozzi opposed religious education in the form of the catechetical method, which constrained the child to the limits of the already defined idea upon which he is requestioned. The catechism was framed in terms of questions and answers each of which contained a religious truth or principle. Theoretically the child was to memorize the question and answer and by so doing internalize the religious principle contained in the answer. This kind of education was regarded by Pestalozzi as devitalized verbalism and memorization. Furthermore, the catechism was geared to a defense of the faith through which the immature member of the particular denomination was to be made firm in religious commitment and also prepared to dispute with those who were antagonistic to the doctrines of the particular denomination. Pestalozzi feared that such an approach would produce contention and conflict rather than lead to the humanitarianism based on the love relationship.

In his account of the school at Bonnal in *Leonard and Gertrude*, Pestalozzi argued against the idle verbalism of mouth religion. The good pastor did not allow children to learn dogma by rote memorization since this method divided Christians against each other. Instead of using preachment and admonition the pastor cooperated with the village schoolmaster in training the children for a peaceful and industrious vocational life. By developing habits of industry the foundations of a quiet or silent habit of worship of God and of a "pure, active, and silent benevolence to man" were established:

> *The pastor based every word of his brief instructions in religion upon the doings and omissions of the children, their circumstances, and duties in life; so that, when he talked with them of God and eternity, he seemed to be speaking of father and mother, of house and home—of things closely connected with this world.*[8]

Pestalozzi's religious values closely resembled a nonde-nominational, humanitarian, pietistical form of common Christianity that was not unlike that advocated by the American educational reformer Horace Mann. In an age of Protestant-Catholic tensions the Pestalozzian approach to religious education failed to satisfy either of the contending creeds.

AESTHETIC VALUES

Unfortunately Pestalozzi failed to articulate an adequate interpretation of the role of aesthetic values in man's education. His axiological concern was directed to the moral-ethical dimension rather than to the aesthetic realm. Discussion of the aesthetic is complicated by the fact that although Pestalozzi recognized beauty in nature he failed to provide for a method of aesthetic appreciation or expression.

As indicated earlier, Pestalozzi's empathy with nature and the natural had large overtones of romanticism. Nature appeared to man in the form of misty, vague, cloudy sense impressions. The Pestalozzian model of man was the harmoniously balanced and integrated personality. Such a wholistic view of man was based on a sense of aesthetic proportion. The concept of the family circle and mother-child love was at times more poetical than descriptive. Pestalozzi, then, appreciated the beautiful as he did the good and the true.

Although appreciating the aesthetic, Pestalozzi's educational method did not emphasize aesthetic values. Using analysis and reductionism he found man to be a creature possessing moral, intellectual, and physical powers. Instruction was reduced to the elements of sound, form, and number. Although a continuum human experience was broken down into finely detailed gradations, phases, and steps. The aesthetic experience, in contrast, is a unified experience by which man as perceiver feels the wholeness and unity of the aesthetic object, not as parts, but as a totality. Although the Pestalozzian model of man was such a wholistic harmony, the method worked out for his development emphasized analysis rather than synthesis.

Pestalozzi approached artistic education as a means of educating the senses and the physical powers. The senses of sight and sound were to be trained as the necessary physical elements of aesthetic perception. In combination with the mechanical powers of hand and speech, sight and sound were necessary in the production of aesthetic objects. When picture books were used instructionally the pictures were to make the child familiar with the objects represented prior to spelling rather than to stimulate aesthetic appreciation. Music was taught as an aid to moral education. Exercises were devised for the learning of notes according to their length. Notes were sung repeatedly in order to concentrate on timing; then different notes were sung to concentrate on tone. By means of combination a rhythmic sentence, a succession of notes arranged in order of time, was incorporated with a melodic sentence, a succession of notes incorporated in order of tone. In limiting instruction to vocal music Pestalozzi stressed melody, harmony, tempo, and the reading and composing of songs.[9]

INTELLECTUAL VALUES

Since Pestalozzi's psychologizing of instruction according to a natural method of education has been treated in Chapters IV and V, the discussion of intellectual values will not again deal with cognition or the education of the intellectual powers. Rather the intellectual values will be considered from the perspective of the total product of education, the harmoniously integrated natural man. Man's intellectual values are based on his perception of reality. If man lacks cognitive skill in forming clear concepts from sense impression, his ideas will remain cloudy, confused, and inaccurate. Without a clear apprehension of reality judgment is impaired as man acts on the basis of erroneous evidence. If man has received a natural education that cooperated with his powers of cognition, then the possibilities for forming correct judgments are enhanced.

The intellectual values, too, need to be structured around a core of natural priorities. Pestalozzi attacked the artificialities that were caused by an emphasis on one-sided verbal abstractions. An unnatural, artificially educated man might misconstrue the intellectual values as referring to such abilities as expertise in abstraction, disputation and argument, syllogistic reasoning, or philosophical and theological speculation. For Pestalozzi intellectual development did not lie in these artificial skills, which were separated from earning a living or loving one's neighbor.

The intellectual values were interpenetrated by both the moral values and the physical or practical values. Moral sensibility, nurtured in earliest childhood by the love relationship, gave direction to man's intellectual powers. Natural education, in fact, depended upon the climate of emotional security. Only in such an environment was it possible for education to proceed according to nature. The mental powers were not merely abstractive but were combined with the practical powers. Although the intellectual and the physical were separate powers they had a common source and culminated in common action. Like Dewey, Pestalozzi did not separate existentially theory and practice, thinking and doing. Thought culminated in action. Nor was the moral intention of the doer separated from the action; the doer was morally responsible for the deed.

Although most of Pestalozzi's educational writings dealt with the special method of form, language, and number, the general method, the climate of emotional security, was necessary for the proper functioning of the special method. In terms of bulk most of the natural method was devoted to the training of the cognitive powers of man and hence to intellectual education. The spirit of Pestalozzianism, as distinct from the form, contained much that was anti-intellectual, if intellectualism is construed as verbal, abstractive, or literary.

PHYSICAL VALUES

Pestalozzi recognized no existential separation of theory and practice, thought and action. The natural man was a person whose moral, intellectual, and physical powers were fully developed and harmoniously blended. The physical values embraced the entire complex of specific bodily movements, practical abilities, and specific kinds of vocational activities. These physical, practical, and vocational values were influenced by both the moral and intellectual values that gave them direction. When Pestalozzi first embarked on an educational career at Neuhof, his overriding concern was that all men, particularly the poor, should be trained to exercise the skills needed for earning a living. Although he turned to more extensive theorizing about cognitive learning later at Burgdorf and Yverdon, he retained his interest in physical and vocational education. Such practical education was necessary in making each individual economically self-sufficient. Extensive programs of practical education were needed if men were to cope successfully with the economic and social changes wrought by the industrial revolution. Although Pestalozzi recognized the necessity for a program of practical education, he always urged the integration of the vocational values with an harmonious orchestration of moral and intellectual values. The natural man was to be educated primarily as a human being and then, and only then, for a particular occupation or profession.

Physical education began with the child's power of movement, which required the same careful exercise as the power of thought. The humane impulse of the heart and the constructive thought of the mind were inadequate without culmination in action. Man as a doer needed specific training so that the body would be healthy, strong, and dexterous. Beginning with the child's rudimentary movements of hands and feet, Pestalozzi fashioned an ABC of Physical Actions by which children progressed from simple to more complicated activities. Such a gradation of physical activities was believed to contain the foundations of the most complicated forms of human practical abilities. Striking, carrying, thrusting, throwing, drawing, turning, encircling, and swinging contained the foundations of all possible actions. These physical exercises were to be harmoniously arranged in compatibility with the exercises of sound, form, and number teaching.[10] Such basic exercises were to proceed from general bodily control, to particular skills, and then to an understanding of the underlying principles of physical power and its practical use.

Although the art of gymnastics constituted the formal program of physical education, the physical values were also cultivated by the informal range of physical activities. Through hikes, excursions, swimming, climbing, games, and play, the child's physical and social skills and experiences were broadened. Gardening integrated physical exercise with a basic vocational skill. Although he followed his methodological bent to reductionism and analyzed movement into a series of graduated exercises, Pestalozzi provided numerous informal occasions for developing physical skills.

VOCATIONAL EDUCATION

Pestalozzi's first educational venture, at Neuhof, was based on a conception of the school as a combination of the home and the workshop. In such a dual-purpose institution the emotional-intellectual values could be cultivated in the home context and the physical-vocational values were to be cultivated in the workshop aspect of the school. Such a dualistic approach would integrate the intellectual, the moral, and the physical powers of man into a harmony.

Vocational education embraced two phases: the cultivation of the physical powers and the fitting of these powers to particular situations. The cultivation of the physical powers flowed in a continuum from man's ability to move and to act. Pestalozzi defined the power of the hand, or doing, as that which "gives expression to the products of the human intellect and the impulses of the heart by means of which all the skills needed for domestic and civil life must be developed." [11] Synonymous with physical exercises vocational education embraced the development of all man's physical powers. From elementary gymnastics to complicated movements every stage was to be completed and perfected before embarking on the next stage.

The perfected physical movements were then fitted to the performance of specific tasks or to work. Pestalozzi did not believe that work was harmful to the child. Rather it was beneficial since meaningful work activities provided the occasions for combining action with morality and intelligence. If the work tasks were to be fulfilled efficiently the worker needed to combine action with intelligent planning and a willingness or desire to accomplish them.

Work depended on the fitting of the physical movement into the context of the specific environmental condition or situation. The child's immediate environment contained occasions for work that related to the family's economic needs. Children as part of the family circle were included in helping the family support itself. If children were exercised in the tasks occurring in the environment, they would then become acquainted with skills needed for the particular social and economic station occupied by the family. According to Pestalozzi the most efficient parents were those who were educated for earning a living in their particular station of life. Although often called a social and political reformer Pestalozzi did not stress social and economic mobility. Education was not a means for enabling individuals to move to a higher socioeconomic level. Rather vocational education should function within a context of situational appropriateness. Appropriate kinds of vocational preparation for various individuals depended upon their station in life.

Although there were many kinds of vocational situations and a corresponding number of appropriate training programs, Pestalozzian vocational education was divided into three major work areas: agriculture, handicrafts, and industry. Although concerned with vocational education it should be remembered that Pestalozzi always subordinated such work to general education. Vocational education was merely a means to the education of the natural man. In writing of the agricultural and industrial work done at Neuhof, Pestalozzi said:

> *But, however much I felt that my institution required this, I was no less convinced that every vocational training which did not provide the individual with a commensurate cultivation of the head and the heart would not only be inadequate but would be unworthy and would degrade him to the status of one slavishly trained merely for making a living.*[12]

Pestalozzi's division of vocational endeavor into agriculture, handicraft production, and industry should be interpreted within the context of the Swiss situation during the early stages of the nineteenth-century industrial revolution. Agriculture remained an essential support of the

Swiss economy. Pestalozzi himself attempted to earn his fortune through scientific agriculture. Although failing as a practical farmer Pestalozzi regarded agriculture as a desirable occupation from two theoretical points of view. First, farming provided a closeness to the soil that brought man face to face with his natural environment. In this intimacy with nature artificial contrivances and idle pursuits were irrelevant. Second, Pestalozzi was influenced by the economic doctrines of the pre-Revolutionary physiocrats that held all economic value to be based on land. In terms of practical pedagogy, gardening and animal husbandry provided excellent occasions for the integration of the heart, head, and hands in meaningful work.

Somewhat more complicated was Pestalozzi's view of handicraft production and factory work. Both of these were actually stages in the processes of the industrial revolution. In countries, such as Switzerland, that had an essentially agricultural economy prior to industrialization the industrial revolution went through two phases: home industries in which families worked in the production of handicrafts; the factory system, which because of mass production became a more efficient means of producing industrial products. Although aware that industrialization was bringing about great social changes, Pestalozzi did not fully realize that the stage of home industry was a temporary phase of the movement that would eventuate in factories. Part of his inability to recognize the broader aspects of this movement might have resulted from the unique Swiss situation, which managed to preserve a large part of handicraft production in home industry.

Just as the first occasions for the development of the moral and intellectual powers occurred within the family

circle, the home provided the first occasions for the exercise of work activities. Although the rising tide of industrialization weakened home industry Pestalozzi believed
that domestic training and handicraft production were
worth preserving. Pestalozzi was apprehensive that factory
industry might have a detrimental effect on the working
population since it weakened the home as a place of fam-
ily-centered work. He believed that "home happiness,
home industry, and home manners" were the best means
of averting the dehumanizing tendencies of the factory
system.

To appreciate his view of home industry it is necessary
to recall Pestalozzi's account of the home of Gertrude and
Leonard in the village of Bonnal. Here education began in
the living room. Since work was essential for the common people the entire day was planned. There was no
time for leisure or idleness. Every child was trained to
contribute to the family by working with the objects and
performing the skills appropriate to the family's welfare.
Pestalozzi's picture of Gertrude's home rested on the
strong notion that children were to share in providing for
the economic necessities of the family. If given responsibilities children would learn to be economically self-
sufficient and avoid sinking into the class of the dependent
poor or poverty ridden.

Gluelphi, the schoolmaster of Bonnal, also made a close
connection between formal education and vocational
training. The teacher was well acquainted with all man-
ner of house and field labor so as to be able to provide
correct vocational training. The well-educated man must
learn to practice skillfully what is to be his future occupation. Since the chief occupations in the vicinity of Bonnal

were farming and factory work, good school practice was based on what the particular children were to do in later life.

Although clearly preferring home occupations Pestalozzi provided for the education of factory workers. The factory tended to replace the home as the actual place of work in the industrialized environment. Therefore the school took on greater obligations in the education of the young since the home no longer possessed the possibilities for work that it had exercised in a more agricultural environment. With industrialization, such as cotton manufacturing, the child as a worker remained for long periods of time in the factory where he performed the same standardized tasks and had slight experience in other activities. The school had to enlarge its functions by introducing the child to the broader range of work activities. In addition to vocational training the school had to educate factory workers in the values of efficiency, thrift, cleanliness, and orderliness. Mothers needed instruction in proper child care. To avoid dissipation through idleness and drinking, factory workers needed instruction on planning for financial security. Pestalozzi's great concern was that although industrialization was producing more wealth, this increased wealth was being wasted on the wrong things.

SOCIAL VALUES

Although Pestalozzi did not refer directly to the social values, he accepted the premise that man was a social being as well as a natural product. While the area of social val-

ues was not identified particularly, the moral, intellectual, and physical values held great implications for the
socialization process. Morality was based on man's obligations and duties to others. The love relationships by definition required both a lover and a loved one. If Pestalozzi
had structured a desired world order it might have resembled Comenius' pansophist world community where each
man loved his brothers. In discussing education in the
context of social values, the following Pestalozzian attitudes might be identified: the right of each man to receive
a natural education; the appropriateness of the kind of
education each man should be given in terms of his socioeconomic class.

Pestalozzi believed that human nature was everywhere
the same and was defined by the essential moral, intellectual, and physical powers that were uniform to all men.
Every man should have the right to have his natural
powers developed through the natural method of education based on language, form, and number. Thus there
was a natural equality underlying all men as members of
the human race. Pestalozzi regarded education as one of
the natural rights of man. As such it should be available to
all regardless of social conditions since every man ought to
be morally, intellectually, and physically well developed.

Despite the general uniformity of all men as based on
the underlying powers of human nature, Pestalozzi believed that there was also an appropriate education that
ought to be given to each man in terms of his station in
life. The doctrine of appropriateness was based on Pestalozzi's view of society. Each man was born into a socioeconomic class and there he was to remain. Each man should

perform the particular duties and obligations relevant to his station in life to the best of his ability and be content to do so. This view of appropriateness may have arisen in part from Pestalozzi's acceptance of the kind of political paternalism that was associated with the theories of enlightened despotism still current in post-Revolutionary Europe.

Divergences in circumstances necessitated variations in the education of different social classes. The wealthy child needed development in the direction of leadership and paternalism. The poor child needed greater experience in practical work affairs. Both the child of the rich and of the poor needed a balanced use of all their powers. Thus through a combination of the general method and specific vocational training, the balanced and harmonious use of all human powers would occur.[13]

Pestalozzi did not attach significance to social class rivalries or antagonisms. If men were educated with an awareness of their mutual obligations within a context of humanitarian life, they would see that the security and welfare of all classes were interrelated. The upper classes were to be paternalistic in their love for the lower classes and the lower classes were to be skillful and industrious in their occupations. The best features of both the upper and lower classes were exhibited by the middle class who had only a small share of material goods but who possessed a great deal of organizational skill, working ability, and persistence. All three social classes were necessary links in the great chain of humanity.

It should be pointed out that although Pestalozzi recognized the existence of socioeconomic classes he was not really concerned with the classes and masses. His educational reforms were not centered in the regeneration of society by means of the group. He believed that reform rested ultimately on the proper education of individuals. He stressed the concept of the individual human being as a distinct and separate entity. To be sure, each man had social obligations, but the primary obligation was that of developing his own uniquely human personality.

EDUCATION OF THE POOR

Pestalozzi was a thorough humanitarian who loved his fellow man. From his earliest days at Neuhof until the climax of his educational career at Yverdon, he hoped to devote himself to the education of the poor. Although he tried on numerous occasions to provide education for paupers and orphans, it was the middle class who were most attracted to the Pestalozzian institutions.

Pestalozzi was sympathetic to the plight of the poor and believed their deprivation resulted from the lack of a natural education. Verbalistic, artificial education had the most detrimental effects upon poor children who were educated neither as harmonious natural men nor as efficient workers. The social changes brought about by the wars of revolution and by industrialization further debilitated the poor. However Pestalozzi did not believe that poverty was a punishment from God or a sign of evil. Rather it resulted from ignorance of natural education and from a distorted environment that had produced distorted individuals.

Pestalozzi's design for the education of the poor was to effect their rehabilitation through natural education rather than continuing charity. Philanthropy without regeneration only contributed to the weakening of the moral condition of the poverty ridden. The initial charity was to be coupled with education so that the individual would be improved and taught to be economically self-sufficient. In stressing that the poor should be educated to support themselves Pestalozzi believed that institutions for their education should center on industry. In his stress on educating the children of the poor in the trades in which they would be expected to work, Pestalozzi revealed himself to be a humanitarian liberal. His thinking in this respect conformed to the pattern of late eighteenth- and early nineteenth-century thought, which emphasized that the children of the poor should learn a useful trade in order not to form a class of permanently impoverished wards dependent upon charity for their existence.

Pestalozzi devoted himself to the regeneration of the lives of the poor through a natural system of education. The cause of poverty was the deprived environment, which could be remedied through education. Furthermore, an education designed to educate poor children needed to imitate their future condition in its organization. The teachers of the poor should be recruited from among the poor themselves and given special teacher training predicated upon the principles of natural education. Pestalozzi was always interested in recruiting young men who might become skilled teachers of the poor. Natural education and teacher training were interdependent emphases in the Pestalozzian institute at Yverdon. The most effective education of the poor as well as all other classes of men was to return to the principles of nature and to psychologize instruction so that all men might learn. In returning to natural principles Pestalozzi soundly condemned the conventional patterns of verbalism:

> *We cannot hide from ourselves that the lowest Christian people of our continent must in many places, sink into these depths, because we, in its lower schools, for more than a century, have given to empty words a weight in the human mind, that not only hindered attention to the impressions of nature, but even destroyed man's inner susceptibility to these impressions.*[14]

· NOTES ·

1. Johann H. Pestalozzi, "Views and Experiences," in Lewis F. Anderson, ed., *Pestalozzi* (New York: McGraw-Hill, 1931), p. 112.
2. *Ibid.*
3. Kate Silber, *Pestalozzi: The Man and His Work* (London: Routledge and Kegan Paul, 1960), pp. 252–253.
4. Pestalozzi, "Views and Experiences," in Anderson, *op. cit.*, pp. 117–118.
5. Silber, *op. cit.*, pp. 41–42.
6. Sister Mary Romana Walch, *Pestalozzi and the Pestalozzian Theory of Education: A Critical Study* (Washington: The Catholic University Press, 1952), p. 58.
7. Pestalozzi, "Why Schools Are a Necessity," in Anderson, *op. cit.*, pp. 122–123.
8. Pestalozzi, *Leonard and Gertrude,* in Henry Barnard, ed., *Pestalozzi and Pestalozzianism* (New York: Brownell, 1862), p. 660.

9. Walch, *op. cit.*, pp. 137–138.
10. Johann H. Pestalozzi, *How Gertrude Teaches Her Children* (Syracuse: Bardeen, 1900), p. 177.
11. Walch, *op. cit.*, p. 102.
12. Pestalozzi, "Views and Experiences," in Anderson, *op. cit.*, pp. 101–102.
13. Silber, *op. cit.*, p. 243.
14. Pestalozzi, *How Gertrude Teaches, op. cit.*, p. 113.

·VII·
Pestalozzianism Assessed

After his death in 1827 Pestalozzi's educational theory was carried throughout Europe by his former teaching assistants. The European and American educators who had visited Yverdon also brought home with them their conception of Pestalozzi's work. Frequently the Pestalozzianism that they carried to their homelands was an inadequate version of the original. Since Pestalozzi's educational theory and practice was a many-sided, loosely organized pedagogical structure, some of the latter-day Pestalozzians saw only a part of this complex structure and their work was handicapped by this limited perspective. In assessing the Pestalozzian influence it must be remembered that the most important phase of the general method lies in the cultivation of a climate of emotional security. Pestalozzi actually was a gentle man, a lover of humanity, and a father to the children who entered his institutes at Neuhof, Stans, Burgdorf, and Yverdon. Unfortunately not all of the followers of Pestalozzi were psychologically suited to fulfill the role of father to humanity. Many of the later Pestalozzians failed to understand that the method demanded the full implementation of the love climate prior to the exercise of the special method in the teaching of subjects and skills. As has been the case with most educational innovations and experiments, once the dedicated originator passes from the scene the work is carried on by individuals who lack his insight.[1] When the guiding spirit of the reform is gone the practice of the method becomes increasingly formalized and devitalized. Such was the case with Pestalozzianism.

IN GERMANY

During the nineteenth century Pestalozzianism was introduced into Prussia. The German philosopher Fichte provided the original stimulus by arguing for the adoption of Pestalozzianism in his *Addresses to the German Nation* in 1808. The Prussian government included elements of Pestalozzian practice in its educational reorganization of 1809. As a result of their exposure to the institute at Yverdon, the famous German educators Froebel and Herbart were aware of and stimulated by Pestalozzi's theory. Although Pestalozzianism had a significant impact upon the German schools, the major emphasis in this assessment of

Pestalozzi's theory is directed to England and the United States.

A number of English visitors came to Yverdon to study Pestalozzi's educational reforms. Andrew Bell, an Anglican clergyman who claimed to be the inventor of the monitorial system of education, had visited Yverdon in 1816. He was critical of what he saw and claimed that his method was far superior. In order to make his method known to the English-speaking world, Pestalozzi wrote a number of letters to the English educator J. P. Greaves, which were translated as *Letters on Early Education*. Although references were made to intellectual and physical education, the *Letters* emphasized the need for the cultivation of a love relationship between mother and child.[2]

Unfortunately the English Pestalozzians, under the influence of Charles and Elizabeth Mayo, lost sight of the cultivation of the love environment of the general method. Charles Mayo, a clergyman, and his sister, Elizabeth, founded a school for upper class children at Cheam Surrey in 1826. Although the first teachers were Swiss the school later resembled a typical English preparatory school. The Mayos attracted the most attention as the proponents of Pestalozzianism in the English-speaking world and founded the Home and Colonial School Society in 1836 to propagandize their version of Pestalozzianism. The society established a model school and normal school in London that trained teachers according to the Mayos'

version of Pestalozzianism. In losing sight of the general
method the Mayos' version emphasized only one phase of
Pestalozzianism, the object lesson, as is illustrated by the
following lesson on glass:

> TEACHER: What is this which I hold in my hand?
> CHILDREN: A piece of glass.
> TEACHER: Can you spell the word glass?
> *(The teacher then writes the word "glass" upon the
> slate, which is thus presented to the whole class as the
> subject of the lesson.)*
> You have all examined this glass; what do you observe?
> What can you say it is?
> CHILDREN: It is bright.
> TEACHER:
> *(Teacher having written the word "qualities" writes
> under it—It is bright.)*
> Take it in your hand and feel it.
> CHILDREN: It is cold.
> *(Written on the board under the former quality.)* [3]

The preceding object lesson developed by Elizabeth
Mayo was one of a series of lesson plans on common objects. When Pestalozzi wrote of sense impression as the
source of all ideas, he did not intend that his principles of
natural education should be so distorted as to become a
mechanical, rote, catechetical affair in which students
replied to a number of previously set questions. The formal
object lesson became a corruption of Pestalozzi's theory.
Unfortunately it could be used quite handily by pedes-
trian practitioners who erroneously believed themselves to
be educational innovators and reformers. Thus the highly
verbal conventional lesson made an inroad into and subverted Pestalozzi's intention of liberalizing educational
practice.

IN THE UNITED STATES

Pestalozzianism in the United States experienced three major waves of interest: (1) the short-lived work of Neef and Maclure at New Harmony, Indiana; (2) the efforts of Barnard; (3) inclusion into the teacher program of Sheldon at Oswego, New York. These three phases of Pestalozzianism in the United States were disconnected episodes rather than sequential stages in a continuing movement.

In 1806 the American geologist-philanthropist, William Maclure, persuaded Joseph Neef, a former teaching assistant at Burgdorf, to emigrate to the United States and establish a Pestalozzian school. From 1809 until the establishment of New Harmony Neef conducted a number of short-lived schools in Philadelphia, in Delaware County, Pennsylvania, and in Louisville, Kentucky. None of them were successful; however, Neef attempted to popularize Pestalozzi to Americans and wrote a *Sketch of a Plan and Method of Education,* in 1808, and *The Method of Instructing Children Rationally in the Arts of Writing and Reading,* in 1813. Although he emphasized the object lesson Neef was aware of and loyal to the major principles of Pestalozzian theory. In writing of Pestalozzi's work, Neef said:

> His pupil always sets out from the known and plain, and proceeds with slow speediness to the yet unknown and complicated. He leaves no point behind him without being perfectly master of it. Every point of knowledge which he acquires is but a step to acquire a new one. All

his faculties are displayed; but none is overstrained. All his proceedings are subject to the minutest gradation.[4]

In 1825 Neef was called to New Harmony to take charge of the Pestalozzian school that was to be an educational center in the utopian community established by Robert Owen and William Maclure in southern Indiana. Internal strife and the financial disputes between the cofounders caused the utopian experiment to collapse. Although New Harmony was a fascinating episode in American social history, its total impact was slight. By 1828 the Owenite community had disintegrated. It is significant to note that Pestalozzianism was first introduced into the United States not only as an educational reform but to contribute to a broader communitarian social reform.[5]

During his long lifetime from 1811 until 1900 Henry Barnard served the American common school in a variety of capacities. He was the commissioner of schools in Connecticut, edited the *Connecticut Common School Journal* from 1838 to 1842, served as the first United States Commissioner of Education, and published and edited the *American Journal of Education* from 1856 to 1881. In his work of winning support for the establishment of the common school, Barnard popularized Pestalozzianism. Having traveled in Europe he was familiar with the work of Pestalozzi. In his conduct of teacher institutes Barnard gave several lectures on Pestalozzi's educational theory and practice. After having published a number of essays on Pestalozzi's work, he collected them into a comprehensive volume, *Pestalozzi and Pestalozzianism,* published in

1859 and reprinted in 1862. This work included three sections: the life and educational system of Pestalozzi, selections from Pestalozzi's publications, and public instruction in Switzerland.[6]

Barnard's contribution to Pestalozzianism in the United States was his popularization of the theory among American educators. His interest was a more pervasive and significant source of Pestalozzianism than the New Harmony experiment. He was part of a New England educational circle composed of individuals, such as Amos Bronson Alcott, William C. Woodbridge, and William Russell, who were aware of Pestalozzian theory and tried to incorporate it into their own educational enterprises.[7] The major work of this group consisted in their educational writing and in their limited experiments.

The work of Edward A. Sheldon, 1823–1897, and his associates at the Oswego Normal School constituted the third major phase of the Pestalozzian movement in the United States.[8] Sheldon, the superintendent of the normal school, introduced the narrow English conception of the formal object lesson into teacher education. The basic operating principle at Oswego was that all knowledge derived from sense perception and that all instruction should be based on real objects. Sheldon and his associates, Margaret Jones, formerly a teacher in the Mayos' Home and Colonial Training School, and Herman Krusi, Jr., the son of one of Pestalozzi's teaching assistants, worked out an extensive program of teacher preparation that was based on the object lesson. Like Elizabeth Mayo, Sheldon published books of lesson plans based on the sensory examination of a number of common objects. Unfortunately the lessons on glass, water, and coal were very formalized and followed the prestructured, question and answer approach developed by the Mayos. The Oswego approach to object teaching attracted attention among American educators and in 1865 the National Teacher's Association Committee on Object Teaching reported:

> *Whenever this system has been confined to elementary instruction and has been employed by skillful, thorough teachers, in unfolding and disciplining the faculties, in fixing the attention and awakening thought, it has been successful.*[9]

The work of Sheldon and the Oswego Normal School must be viewed from two perspectives: the contribution to American common-school teaching and teacher preparation; the contribution to the Pestalozzian movement in the United States. Oswego's existence undoubtedly improved the quality of common-school teachers and their teaching. Although the Oswego object lesson was highly formal it was nevertheless an improvement over the memorization of highly verbal materials. The object lesson plan organized instruction to the degree that the teacher could exercise greater planning and control in the classroom. The Oswego method, however, was not really natural education as had been practiced by Pestalozzi. It was rather the extension of the formalized English object lesson into American pedagogy. Although this lesson was attributed to Pestalozzi it is doubtful if the man of Burgdorf and Yverdon would have recognized it. Although the English-American object teachers gave lip service to sense experience, their lessons came to contain long lists of definitions or facts about the object under study. The process of verbalization and memorization that Pestalozzi so vehemently opposed subverted object teaching.

While the work of Neef, Barnard, and Sheldon constituted the three best known phases of Pestalozzianism in the United States, the spirit of Pestalozzi could be found in the work of the American progressive educators of the late nineteenth and early twentieth centuries. Educational reformers such as Colonel Francis Parker, Junius Meriam, Marietta Johnson, and others sought to liberalize American pedagogy. Led by Stanwood Cobb, the Progressive Education Association was organized in 1918. Emphasizing the interests and needs of the child, the educational progressives advocated: (1) child freedom based upon natural development; (2) direct experience with the world and its activities; (3) the use of the senses in training pupils in observation and judgment; (4) cooperation between the school and home and between parents and teachers.[10] Pestalozzi would have felt much at home in the company of the child-centered progressives who were prescribing many of the same reforms for twentieth-century schools that he himself had urged in the nineteenth century.

If he would have been welcomed in the Progressive Education Association, Pestalozzi also would have approved of John Dewey's urging that all learning should originate in the learner's experience. With their mutual stress on experience, there was a strong relationship between Pestalozzi and Dewey. While Pestalozzi emphasized that all instruction should begin in the home circle and proceed from the child's immediate to the more distant environment, Dewey stressed an experiential continuum in which the learner's past experience should flow in an unbroken stream into his present situation. In his schools at Stans, Burgdorf, and Yverdon, Pestalozzi engaged his students in activities arising in the immediate environment. At the University of Chicago Laboratory School that he founded in 1896, Dewey also sought to involve his students in cooperative and socially useful living. Although Dewey's Instrumentalism differs philosophically from Pestalozzi's obscure naturalism, the emphasis on the learner's interests, needs, and experiences was a pedagogical principle mutually shared by both educators.

In attacking an education that was excessively verbal and purely abstract and theoretical, Pestalozzi, like Rousseau, was a forerunner of such activity-oriented educators as William Heard Kilpatrick. Through the project method of education, Kilpatrick sought to engage students in full participation in the learning situation. In attacking bookishness, verbalism, and memorization, both Kilpatrick and Pestalozzi preferred the man who was a wholehearted doer rather than the disinterested scholar who was a sophisticated speculator into the nature of things.

In the spirit of Pestalozzianism, the American progressive educators did battle with the fortresses of memorization, abstraction, and verbalization that were the pedantic defenses of the traditional school. Although only one of many influences on progressivism, Pestalozzi's general method, which was based on the cultivating of an environment of emotional security, greatly resembled the American progressive's permissive solicitude of the interests and needs of the child. Unfortunately for both the nineteenth-century Pestalozzi and the twentieth-century progressive, the traditional school was a mighty fortress in which the teaching of the three R's was guarded against change. Rather than bringing about a sweeping educational revolution, the work of the reforming Pestalozzi and the later progressives secured limited changes that were gradually incorporated into the fabric of conventional schooling. The greatest contribution of these educational reformers was to set in motion forces that led to the very gradual transformation of the school rather than to its sweeping reformation.

CRITIQUE

Although there has been a continuing assessment of Pestalozzi's theories and practices throughout this book, a few final words might be said in assessing the influence of the Swiss educator. As has been mentioned, Pestalozzi's lack of consistency and his unsystematic theorizing were detrimental to the whole educational edifice which he sought to construct. His basic concepts, such as *Anschauung,* element, psychologizing, and even natural education were cloudy terms. He gave them multifaceted definitions that diminished their effectiveness in the hands of his followers.

Despite this weakness Pestalozzi's major contribution was natural education, which included a reverence for child nature and a consideration of child experience in relationship to environment. His rejection of child corruption was based on his view of man as being naturally good.

This meant that he believed that childhood was uniquely precious and valuable to each man. Early childhood education, in particular, was essential in developing the proper attitudes and values. His general method, the creation of a love environment, was much ahead of its time as Pestalozzi anticipated the course of modern child psychology. The doctrines of the child-centered school and child permissiveness had their origins at Neuhof, Stans, Burgdorf, and Yverdon. Therefore one of Pestalozzi's significant contributions was his enlightened view of child nature.

Although the general method was a major contribution, Pestalozzi's special method, defined here as the teaching of subjects and skills, left much to be desired. His reductionism of simple to complex, near to far, and specific to general was based on a confusion of the logically simple and the psychologically simple. His propensity to analyze all instruction into elements caused him to reduce some of his sound lessons into the memorization of sets of nonsense syllables and to reduce physical exercises into eccentric and meaningless movements.

The valuable part of the special method rested on its relationship to the child's experience. Pestalozzi, like Dewey, insisted that the continuity of experience be maintained. As the home circle led to the school the child's experience was unbroken by the intrusion of adult experience in the form of abstract ethical or literary materials. Such an intrusion of materials would lack meaning for the child who, if coerced, would memorize rather than understand. Pestalozzi's stress on maintaining a continuum of experience caused him to examine and to use the learning possibilities that existed in the child's immediate environment. When used in an experiential context related to environment, Pestalozzi's principles of from the simple to the complex and from the near to the far were valuable additions to educational practice.

Although he considered that education could advance the cause of social reform, such reformation always resulted from individual effort. While he recognized the sociological implications of education, his role as a social reformer seems exaggerated. Developing no detailed political or sociological theories for social reformation, he relied almost exclusively on educational processes to bring man to the utopia of the moral state. At times, however, he was able to render an accurate reading of the political and industrial events of his time. Although aware that the industrial revolution and the extension of citizenship would necessitate a new method of education, his own system was not particularly geared to either the requirements of industry or citizenship. He seemed to rely more on man's benevolent paternalism as a means of social regeneration than on a scheme for planned social change. Although an educational innovator Pestalozzi was really more a political and social conservative than a radical revolutionary.

In terms of the axiological dimension of education Pestalozzi's model of man who harmoniously developed his moral, intellectual, and physical powers was suited for life in any age. Fearing the effects of industrial specialization and the growth of a dehumanized mass society, he cultivated the model of the generally educated man. Certainly his stress on the integrated natural man in the context of the moral state was a desirable educational outcome. Despite some of the methodological eccentricities that crept into the special method, he never lost his vision of the natural man.

Finally something must be said about Pestalozzi's basic humanitarianism. As a lover of all mankind he made love the center of his educational theory and practice. Mother love, the loving home circle, and love of man and of God were persistent themes in his writing. In our age, which tends to base educational ends on statistically quantified empirical results, Pestalozzi's emphasis on man's need to be a lover may sound simplistic and archaic. Despite its confused terminology and its meticulously graduated exercises, the Pestalozzian philosophy of education was essentially a love message in which Papa Pestalozzi told men to simply love one another.

· NOTES ·

1. Broudy and Palmer indicate in *Exemplars of Teaching Method* that many educational reforms have met this fate.
2. Johann H. Pestalozzi, *Letters on Early Education Addressed to J. P. Greaves* (London: Sherwood, Gilbert, and Piper, 1827), pp. 148–149.
3. Elizabeth Mayo, *Lessons on Objects as Given to Children Between the Ages of Six and Eight in a Pestalozzian School* (London: Seeley and Burnside, 1835), pp. 5–6.
4. Joseph Neef, *Sketch of a Plan and Method of Education* (Philadelphia: privately published, 1808), p. 7.
5. The best sources for the history of New Harmony are Arthur E. Bestor, *Backwoods Utopias: The Sectarian and*

Owenite Phases of Communitarian Socialism in America (Philadelphia: University of Pennsylvania Press, 1950), and Bestor, *Education and Reform at New Harmony: Correspondence of William Maclure and Marie Ducles Fretageot* (Indianapolis: Indiana Historical Society, 1948).

6. Henry Barnard, *Pestalozzi and Pestalozzianism* (New York: Brownell, 1862).

7. Will Seymour Monroe, *History of the Pestalozzian Movement in the United States* (Syracuse: Bardeen, 1907), pp. 147–155.

8. For a history of the Oswego phase, see Ned H. Dearborn, *The Oswego Movement in American Education* (New York: Teachers College, Columbia University, 1925).

9. Monroe, *op. cit.*, pp. 183–184.

10. Adolphe E. Meyer, *The Development of Education in the Twentieth Century* (Englewood Cliffs, N.J.: Prentice-Hall, 1949), p. 71.

Index

WESTMAR COLLEGE LIBRARY